DYING
DEATH
and
DESTINY

BY *Herbert Lockyer*

All About Bible Study
All the Apostles of the Bible
All the Books and Chapters of the Bible
All the Doctrines of the Bible
All the Children of the Bible
All the Holy Days and Holidays
All the Kings and Queens of the Bible
All the Men of the Bible
All the Women of the Bible
All the Miracles of the Bible
All the Parables of the Bible
All the Prayers of the Bible
All the Promises of the Bible
All the Trades and Occupations of the Bible
All the Messianic Prophecies of the Bible
All the Divine Names and Titles in the Bible
Death and Life Hereafter
Everything Jesus Taught, 5 vols.
How to Find Comfort in the Bible
Last Words of Saints and Sinners
The Lockyer Bible Preacher's Library, 5 vols.
Seasons of the Lord, 4 vols.
Seven Words of Love
The Man Who Died for Me
The Sins of Saints
Dark Threads the Weaver Needs
Their Finest Hour
Dying, Death, and Destiny

HERBERT LOCKYER

DYING
DEATH
and
DESTINY

Fleming H. Revell Company
Old Tappan, New Jersey

Unless otherwise identified, Scripture quotations are from the King James Version of the Bible.

Scripture quotations identified MOFFATT are from THE BIBLE: A NEW TRANSLATION by James Moffatt. Copyright 1954 by James A. R. Moffatt. By permission of Harper & Row, Publishers, Inc.

Dying, Death and Destiny is based on seven tapes made by Dr. Herbert Lockyer for the Foundation for the Advancement of Christian Evangelism, Colorado Springs, Col. © 1979 by F.A.C.E. World Rights Reserved. Produced in the United States of America. Used by permission. Tapes may be had from the above foundation.

Library of Congress Cataloging in Publication Data

Lockyer, Herbert.
    Dying, death, and destiny.

    1. Death.   I. Title.
BT825.L62   236   80-18089
ISBN 0-8007-1133-5

TO
Mrs. Ruth Weise
and her three noble sons

Contents

Preface

The Foundation for the Advance of Christian Evangelism, Colorado Springs, Colorado, has earned my sincere gratitude by allowing me to put the material in their tapes *On Dying, Death, and Destiny* into printed form. I would urge all believers to use one of their tape albums when visiting the suffering, the dying, and the bereaved.

Because death has passed upon all men, how essential it is, if we have a dying period, to possess the assurance that when we meet this last enemy, it cannot rob us of the life beyond, in which there is no death!

May He "Who was dead, but is alive forever more" be pleased to bless and use this further Revell study for the salvation of both those in health and the dying who, hitherto, have lived without hope of eternal life!

HERBERT LOCKYER

DYING DEATH *and* DESTINY

1

Reason and Reality of Death

While there are some aspects of life more pleasant than others to dwell upon, yet those aspects we may deem unpleasant to think about often prove to be the most profitable. There may be features of life's pilgrimage that are not altogether welcome; nevertheless they are true; and Paul's exhortation reads, ". . . whatsoever things are true. . . think on these things" (Philippians 4:8).

Among these undeniable, somber facts of life are those of death and dying—inescapable events we tend to push into the background of our thinking and action, until grim necessity overtakes us. This is the prime reason why I have undertaken to prepare these messages dealing with dying and death and life beyond the grave. My heartfelt prayer is that God will abundantly bless and use these messages for the honor of His name, both through the enlightenment and assurance of those who are truly His and also through the salvation of many who have been living without hope beyond this mortal life.

Some readers might query my qualifications for dealing with the inevitable end awaiting us all, the imperative need for preparing for the road to death, and our continuance in another world in which there are no graves. First of all, throughout a long pastoral ministry, I had an almost daily contact with the sick, the dying, and the bereaved. This caused me to constantly seek the aid and guidance of the Holy Spirit—the Comforter. Through Him I found strength to pray and talk with those stricken with a fatal illness or accident and to help bring peace to those relatives who buried their dead in God's green acre. Pastors who live and labor in the light of eternity and who believe that Scripture offers the only authentic revelation of the cause and certainty of death—and of the only way to meet it—are under the solemn obligation of emulating the faithful witness of John Bunyan's Interpreter. He not only bore his Great Commission in his look, but also had the law of truth written upon his lips.

My next qualification for covering all subjects associated with dying and death is a most personal, never-to-be-forgotten one that I am somewhat reluctant to describe. During the last six or seven years of our sixty-six years of marriage, my dear wife was practically dead to the world. She became mentally afflicted with no consciousness of past or present, unable even to recognize her dear ones. Speechless and almost blind and deaf and bedridden, she was my daily care and had to be fed like a baby, with baby food. Often, as I looked upon her afflicted, helpless form, I would look up and cry, "Oh, my God, why?" Unashamedly, I confess that often I prayed that, if it was His will, He would take her to be with Himself. At last, one Sunday afternoon, when we were alone, the death throttle—so painful and distressing to hear and watch—came from the throat of my ninety-two-year-old partner. In a few minutes she died in my arms—as my volume *Dark Threads the Weaver Needs* more fully describes. Through such a hard experience I have a more "thoughtful love, through constant watching wise," and a "heart at leisure from itself to soothe and sympathize"—a sentiment I trust this volume will reflect.

Further, personal fitness to meditate upon what dying and

death signify and involve arises from the fact that I am now ninety-three years old and naturally not far away from proving, with the poet Longfellow, that, "There is no death! What seems so is transition." At such an advanced age, one is found to be living more in the light of eternity than ever before, with the things of earth growing dim in the light of His glory and grace. With my face toward sunrise, before long, I shall hear my beloved Saviour say, "Rise, My love, My fair one, and come away." Assured, then, that I shall see my Pilot face-to-face, when I have crossed the bar, eagerness is mine to share with you the comfort of the Scriptures regarding God's care for the dying and the dead and for those bereaved ones who live on, even though half of their hearts are in heaven.

Death Is Real

At the outset of this meditation on the doctrine of last things, I deem it essential to deal with the reality of death itself. In these turbulent days, when death so freely rides the winds of the world, there is scarcely a newspaper or radio report that does not bear some reference to it, whether it comes naturally or by accident, by suicide, murder, or war. Death is always a tragedy to somebody. Never a day passes without death breaking some heart. Never a corner is safe from the dripping rain of death's tears. Death is the skeleton at every feast, the bitterness in every cup, the discord in our music, the nameless dread that has haunted man; it has threatened us since grief had its first birthplace in a mother's broken heart, as she knelt by the side of her boy who had been murdered through the personal violence of his brother. Death never loses its fearful countenance, but remains a tremendous and solemn event all of us have to meet. Ignore it we cannot, seeing it is continually intruding into our circle of loved ones and acquaintances.

Surely then, it is incumbent upon us to discover all we

can of such a prominent incident in life as death, an event as conspicuous as our birth.

> Thou, O Death
> What is thy meaning? Some there are of men
> Deny thee quite. "There is no death" they say.
> But ever with veil'd aspects com'st thou still.
>   AUTHOR UNKNOWN

As soon as we are placed in a cradle, we commence our funeral march to the grave. Joseph Hall, in *Epistles*, wrote, "Death borders upon our birth, and our cradle stands in the grave." Too often, babies die soon after they leave the womb, with the grave quickly following the cradle. Death is with us from our earliest consciousness; and, if, as Solomon reminds us, ". . . the day of death [is better] than the day of one's birth" (Ecclesiastes 7:1), is it not utter foolishness to neglect consideration of all that death involves? We have been reminded that many things may be done by proxy; other things may be bought off and evaded; but we cannot evade our physical dissolution. Each person, whether saint or sinner, must pass through the portal of the tomb:

> Life, in some respects, is like a game of chess. Upon the board, during the progress of the game, the pieces occupy different positions and different values; but when the game is over, all alike, bishop, kings, knights and pawns go into the common box. In life here below, one man is a king, another a bishop, another the master of a great business, another a menial, a mere pawn. But when death comes— the great leveler—all men are equal in the solemn stillness of the sepulchre.

The Bible, God's infallible revelation, states the reason and reality of death in this terse and authoritative way: "Wherefore, as by one man sin entered into the world, and death by sin; and so death passed upon all men, for that all have sinned" (Romans 5:12). Because all have sinned and come short of the glory of God, the soul that sinneth must die (*see* Romans 3:23; 5:12; Ezekiel 18:4, 20).

Although death is inevitable, as the result of sin, we ought not to look upon death with horror, as if it were altogether a monster or robber, waiting to snatch us from all that we cling to in life. While death is a necessary law of nature to which we must submit, it need not be a catastrophe. It is but a stopping place on our journey to the world beyond—a slowing down into the station, not a terminus. According to the natural law of increase, if people never died, this world would not be habitable. Our responsibility is to realize that the date is fixed when we must look death in the face, and a spot is marked where our dust will rest when it returns to its natural abode. At that time the world's ambitions, the strife of tongues, and conflict of passions will float past, as night winds sighing over a deserted shrine.

Queen Elizabeth I of England is said to have cried in her last hour, "All my possessions for a moment of time," but there was no one near to barter with her. Beloved, if we live with our hearts and faces toward sunrise, then, when the Divine Voice says, "It is time to depart," craving will not be ours for further moments of time—for our death will be a birth. As the eyes of a babe open upon the sunlight of earth or as the tiny mass of humanity leaves the darkness of the womb, so when we close our eyes in the darkness of death, we shall open them in a "light that never was on sea or land." I hope to prove, as we come to the truth in these meditations, that death, for the child of God, is not a permanent state, but an art; it is not an abode in which he is to dwell, but a gate to pass through into a richer, fuller life in the world above. There, John assures us, "There is no more death."

Perhaps a fitting conclusion to this, our first consideration of such an important theme, is the way in which the Bible approaches it.

Death Is Sleep

In John 11 it is recorded that, when Martha and her sister, Mary, saw that their brother, Lazarus, was very sick, they sent to Jesus, saying, ". . . Lord, behold, he whom thou lovest is sick" (v. 3). But Jesus' answer appears to be somewhat perplexing, in view of what actually befell Lazarus, for He said, ". . . This sickness is not unto death, but for the glory of God, that the Son of God might be glorified thereby" (v. 4). Lazarus, however, did die as the result of his sickness—a seeming contradiction to our Lord's declaration. The logical explanation is that when He said, ". . . not unto death . . ." He meant not unto a *permanent* state of death. Lazarus would die, but his death would only be a temporary one—as it was. For when he had been dead four days, God and the Lord Jesus were glorified, when Lazarus, still bound in graveclothes, stepped out of his tomb. However before Jesus pronounced the all-commanding words ". . . Lazarus, come forth!" He said to His disciples:

> ". . . Our friend Lazarus sleepeth; but I go, that I may awake him out of sleep." Then said his disciples, "Lord, if he sleep, he shall do well." Howbeit Jesus spake of his death: but they thought that he had spoken of taking of rest in sleep. Then said Jesus unto them plainly, "Lazarus is dead."
>
> John 11:11–14

The Apostle Paul, writing of those who died before the Lord's return, uses the same metaphor for the dead:

> But I would not have you to be ignorant, brethren, concerning them which are asleep. . . . them also which sleep in Jesus will God bring with him. For this we say unto you by

the word of the Lord, that we which are alive and remain
. . . shall not prevent them which are asleep.

1 Thessalonians 4:13–15

Sleep indicates the absence of terror and the presence of repose; hence, ancient believers called their cemeteries *cubiculi*, meaning "sleeping places." Martin Luther once wrote, "A man who is asleep is much like one who is dead." The ancient sages said, "Sleep is the brother of death." Sleep brings rest to the body. In sleep, weariness vanishes, and we rise in the morning—joyous, fresh, and strong. It is thus with death, for the grave is the quiet resting place in which our bodies sleep until the resurrection morn. It must be borne in mind, however, that sleep is only associated with the body, and never with the soul. The Bible clearly asserts continuance of consciousness and activity of the soul after death, ". . . absent from the body, . . . present with the Lord" (2 Corinthians 5:8).

Death Is a Departure

Facing his martyrdom, Paul could write to young Timothy, "For I am now ready to be offered, and the time of my departure is at hand" (2 Timothy 4:6). The term *departure*, we are reminded, literally means "to pull up anchor and set sail." In life, we are anchored to this fleeting world and to material possessions; in death, the anchor is hauled in, and we set sail for the golden shore. John Neale, the famous hymnist, reckoned that his favorite hymn was the one commencing with the line, "Safe home, safe home in port." Tennyson, in his expressive poem "Crossing the Bar," portrays a similar idea.

Death: An Exodus

When Moses and Elijah appeared on the Mount of Transfiguration, we are told that they conversed with Jesus about ". . . his decease which he should accomplish at Jerusalem"

(Luke 9:31). Peter uses the same term for *death:* ". . . after my decease . . ." (2 Peter 1:15). It is common with us to refer to one who has passed away, not as being dead, but as the deceased. The word *decease* actually means a "going out" or "exodus." The second book of the Bible is named Exodus, seeing that it describes the Israelites going out from the bondage of Egypt into liberty—out of a land of anguish and affliction, into a land flowing with milk and honey. Thus is it with death, which is our way out from the partial to the perfect. "For now we see through a glass, darkly; but then face to face . . ." (1 Corinthians 13:12). "The tomb is not a blind alley," wrote Victor Hugo, the brilliant Frenchman. "It is a thoroughfare; it closes in twilight, to open with dawn."

Death: An Exchange

Paul would have us know that death has no terror, seeing that it simply means changing the fragile tent of the body for a more beautiful and eternal covering for the redeemed soul. The mortal body is not a permanent residence, but only a temporary abode, until one is clothed with the resurrection body.

> For we know that if our earthly house of this tabernacle were dissolved, we have a building of God, an house not made with hands, eternal in the heavens. For in this we groan, earnestly desiring to be clothed upon with our house which is from heaven.
>
> 2 Corinthians 5:1, 2

To the believer, death is not a leap in the dark or a gateway into the great unknown, but a quick journey home to Christ, whose glorified body will be the pattern for our deathless new bodies.

2
Distinction Between Death and Dying

In this further aspect of the absorbing theme we are considering, attention must be given to the process of dying, as well as to its end in death. It has been said, "It is not death, but dying, which is terrible." Death must be distinguished from dying, with which it is often confused. For many who know the end is near, the problem is not so much death itself, as the dying, with its hopelessness and helplessness. Death is but the moment when the dying ends. When sufferers are conscious that the gate of death will soon open for them—and often dying patients have an instinctive feeling of this impending decease, an observation relatives who visit them fail to discern—there are several factors that enable the dying to die in dignity and with courage. For instance, the imminent parting from loved ones and the world is somewhat softened for them, if family physicians who cared for them when they were in health are at hand to do everything they can to make their dying easier and more physically comfortable.

Although doctors and nurses are used to seeing patients in a lingering and dying condition and are doubtless amazed at the submissive and brave way in which many face their last enemy—death—one often wonders what their reaction is when a patient asks in a weak and sepulchral voice, "Doctor, is this the end? Is death at hand?" Doubtless, the attitude of the doctor regarding death and of the life to come shapes the answer to such a heartrending question. In her widely read book, *Questions and Answers on Death and Dying,* Dr. Elisabeth Kubler-Ross reveals what the dying have to teach those who contact those patients who maintain some form of hope until they breathe their last. She describes the dying patients' adverse response to those who tell them of their "fatal diagnosis without a chance, without a sense of hope."

A surgeon-friend of mine who lives in Florida recently explained to me his method when, in operating on a patient, he discovers that the chance of survival is nil. He makes a few adjustments that will produce temporary relief and prolong life for a while. Then, when the doomed one is able to receive the verdict, he sits down with him, explains the true nature of the fatal ailment and the impossibility of any immediate or ultimate cure. Being a most sincere Christian, my friend does not stop after the rehearsal of his expert diagnosis. He goes on to kindly point out the necessity of preparing for what lies beyond death. If the patient is a non-Christian, then he sets forth the way of salvation and endeavors to lead the hopeless sufferer into the hope and assurance of a glorious, deathless life beyond the grave. If his patient is a confirmed believer in the Lord Jesus, and if my doctor-friend realizes that the patient's human spirit is conscious that life's pilgrimage is almost over, and if his spirit is composed for the exit from this world—which usually comes quickly—he is thrice happy as the dying saint whispers, "Doctor, all's right for eternity." One can imagine how he would take the hand of the one bound for glory and repeat the lines of Bishop Edward H. Bickersteth:

> Peace, perfect peace, death shadowing us and ours?
> Jesus has vanquished death and all its powers.

Pastors, who augment the comforting ministry of godly physicians and who are usually the first to be notified of a flock member's dying condition, have a most solemn responsibility to discharge—both toward the terminally ill and toward his loved ones and relatives. Any faithful pastor knows that it is not enough to read an appropriate portion of Scripture and then offer a prayer of consolation, before leaving the dying patient. Time must be taken to sit at the bedside and listen to questions—not only regarding personal arrangements as to gifts and legacies and care of loved ones who will be left behind, but also regarding a guilt-laden conscience and how, like the dying thief at Calvary, he can experience forgiveness of past sin and enter upon the life eternal offered to all who believe. This gives the persevering, soul-loving pastor an excellent opportunity of gaining another star for his crown.

The Good Death

If the sufferer is an avowed Christian and has been active for the Master, then, when the crisis comes, death creates no fear or conflict; it is accepted with peace and submission and with the assurance that his Lord awaits to welcome him to Glory, as He did the dying Stephen. If he is too ill to speak, in a silence beyond words and with a composed countenance, one realizes that the dying patient is at peace with God. Alexander Pope, in "The Dying Christian to His Soul," has the lines:

> . . . Trembling, hoping, ling'ring, flying,
> Oh, the pain, the bliss of dying! . . .
> Tell me, my soul, can this be death?

Scripture records the way some conspicuous figures acted in the process of their dying. Jacob, when dying, blessed his two grandsons by Joseph and worshiped God. Joseph, on his deathbed, predicted the severance of Israel from Egypt and gave full instructions as to his final burying place (Genesis 48:15–22; 50:24, 25; Hebrews 11:21, 22). The daughter of Jairus was only twelve years of age when she lay dying.

The distressed father sought the aid of Jesus on behalf of his only child, but Jesus allowed her to die, that, as the Resurrection and the Life, His power might be displayed in her return to life (Luke 8:41–56). Before Stephen fell asleep, as his persecutors sought to stone him to death, he turned his battered, bleeding face to heaven and saw the glory of God and prayed, with a loud voice, for his murderers (Acts 7:54–60).

In the experience of our gracious Lord, distinction is apparent between His dying and His death. For Him, although it was not prolonged, dying was yet most excruciating. As He was being brought into the dust of earth, His strength dried up like a potsherd, and His tongue cleaved to His jaws. Born to die for the world's salvation, His actual dying commenced in the Garden of Gethsemane, where He agonized in prayer and sweated great drops of blood. His soul was exceedingly sorrowful unto death. Then there came the indignities heaped upon Him, such as the smiting of His face, the scourging, the mock coronation with a crown of thorns. Following came the crucifixion itself, with all its dreadful pain and anguish, as the nails were driven through His hands and feet. Coupled with this was the temporary thought that His Father was not near Him in His dying hour. Yet, in dying, He left all His dying saints a wonderful example, in that He thought of others as He faced death. He prayed for His crucifiers, won a dying sinner as the first trophy in this redemptive work, and thought of the future welfare of the mother who had brought Him into the world. Then, when the actual moment of death came, it was quick and triumphant, for, as He died, He cried aloud, "It is finished"; and, as death claimed Him, He surrendered His spirit to God. Glory to His name! It was by His dying and death that He not only slew death, but revealed how His followers could die well. In a spiritual sense, Paul would have us manifest the dying of the Lord Jesus in our daily life (2 Corinthians 4:14–19).

Fear of Dying

Not all the dying can sing the spiritual song R. Slater taught the saints to sing with happy confidence, well over seventy years ago:

> The fear of death is gone forever,
> No more to cause my heart to grieve;
> There is a place, I do believe,
> In Heaven for me beyond the river.

Observation and experience prove that death is not a phantom that the dying feel ashamed to fear. Although we have had the remaking of formulas and efforts to create confidence in dying and the provision of drugs, by medical science, to benumb the mind of the thought of death, the old fear remains. As Dr. Kubler-Ross expresses it:

> Death is still a fearful, frightening happening, and the fear of death is a universal fear even if we think we have mastered it on many levels. The more we are advancing in science, the more we seem to fear and deny the reality of death.

Francis Bacon, the essayist, would have us know that, "Men fear death as children fear to go in the dark," and that, "the pomp of death alarms us more than death itself." You will recall that Shakespeare, in *Measure for Measure*, wrote:

> The weariest and most loathed worldly life
> That age, ache, penury, and imprisonment
> Can lay on nature, is a paradise
> To what we fear of death.

It would seem that, for many, all that they fear—the most dreaded and last—is death. Such fear is worse than death itself. Augustine Hare, an eighteenth-century writer, left us the saying that, "The ancients dreaded death; the Christian can only fear dying." But of all people reaching the end of life, the Christians are those who should not fear dying or death. The last words of Charles Frohman, as he went down to a watery grave when the *Lusitania* sank on 7 May 1915, were, "Why fear death? It is a most beautiful adventure in life."

If, however, one who is dying has not cast his anchor to Christ, the Rock of Ages, he has every reason to be afraid of death and its issue. To die without warning and without Christ as one's personal Saviour is a dreadful end, because a swift and unexpected death means a sudden and eternal separation from God and an eternity of darkness and woe. What they are when they die, unbelievers remain throughout their existence beyond the grave. Solomon reminds us that the ". . . place where the tree falleth, there it shall be" (Ecclesiastes 11:3). This implies a fixity of character and condition.

For a born-again believer, a sudden death means a sudden and eternal glory. Is this not the sum and substance of the blessed Gospel, which declares that Christ came to strip death of its alien terrors? Here is the testimony of Scripture:

> . . . Jesus . . . by the grace of God should taste death for every man. . . . Forasmuch then as the children are partakers of flesh and blood, he also himself likewise took part of the same; that through death he might destroy him that had the power of death, that is, the devil; And deliver them who through fear of death were all their lifetime subject to bondage.
>
> Hebrews 2:9, 14, 15

To these reassuring words we can add those of David in Psalms 23:4: "Yea, though I walk through the valley of the shadow of death, I will fear no evil: for thou art with me. . . ."

One, in dying, conquered death. "He tasted death," or, as the original has it, "deaths." All deaths were rolled into one, and Jesus died that death. He vanquished the devil, who had the power of death, and He expiated the sin that introduced death into God's world. By the cross, the curse has been transmitted into blessing; and death, for the child of God, is but a falling asleep in the arms of Everlasting Love. Thus, the Christian view of death is consoling: The waters once so chill are now warm, the redeemed soul on the way home to God is grateful for them. The fear of death, then, is not something we are left to overcome, but something that has been conquered for us by Another—even by Him who is alive forevermore. Though the reality has to be faced, we do not face it stoically, but as those who know and believe that He who has the keys of death will be our Companion through the dark valley into eternal sunlight. His perfect love will cast out the tormenting fear of death and enable us to depart in peace. May ours be the confidence Henry F. Lyte has enshrined for us in his famous hymn, "Abide With Me."

> I fear no foe, with Thee at hand to bless;
> Ills have no weight, and tears no bitterness.
> Where is death's sting? where, grave, thy victory?
> I triumph still, if Thou abide with me.

3

Three Months to Live

The following letter appeared in the London *Daily Mail*, some time ago. It is a pathetic yet courageous document from a "man of forty" and a solemn appeal to my own heart. It was entitled "Three Months to Live." I herewith quote the whole text of the letter:

If I am not mistaken, there was a picture exhibited a few years ago in which the scene was the consulting-room of a physician who was seated at his desk. Sitting in a chair opposite was a young man who had apparently received his death sentence.

That scene was reconstructed a few days ago, I being the patient sitting opposite the specialist, indeed, the whole scene flashed through my mind as I realized the terrible import of his words.

"We are not infallible, any of us, but as you have demanded the truth I will tell you I do not think that you have more than three or four months to live. There is, of course, such a thing as Nature's miracle, but I do not advise you to rely upon such a remote possibility."

And my feelings? Well, it may seem strange, but after months and months of waiting and doubt, there came almost a feeling of relief. I knew the worst. I had some three months' grace in which I could put my affairs in order before passing into the Great Unknown.

Most people will think it hard for a man of forty, and with plenty of work to do, to be told that he has to go, but it has not struck me in this light. I look around me and see people suffering horribly from various diseases; they would probably welcome death; but my infirmity is not a painful one, nor will its end be painful; so, surely things might be a lot worse.

I shall carry on with my work just as I have done, but I shall probably extract more pleasure from the little things of life than I have done in the past. I mean such things as the beauty of the country in its summer garb, the little things one can so often do to help others, and the gambols of my little colony of cats.

There is, however, one bitter blow. Two people only have I told my tragedy; one a business acquaintance, and the other the sweetest girl who ever breathed, and whom I had hoped to make my partner for life.

It does seem hard to leave her, especially, when, but a year ago, happiness seemed within our grasp. And she, God bless her, cheers me every day by reminding me of the possibility of a Nature's miracle; but I am not sure that this does not make it harder still, as I can see that she refuses to accept the physician's ultimatum.

Maybe there is something in what is called woman's intuition.

Well—I shall know, I expect, before very long.

Three months to live! What a verdict for one to hear who has just reached the prime of life! As you can see, such an ultimatum set this friend thinking about a few things he proposed doing in the short span of life left to him. He is to put his affairs in order before passing into the Great Unknown; carry on with his work, just as he has done; extract more pleasure from the little things of life than he had done in the past, such as the beauty of the country in its summer garb, the gambols of his colony of cats, the doing of those little things helpful to other people.

Making the Most of Our Time

Such a noble resolve on the part of this man who had received his sentence of death aroused my thoughts. I said to myself, *Suppose I had only three months to live; what would I do?* With the belief that Christ may return within the lifetime of those within this present generation, how ought we to spend our lives? Suppose we knew that in three months' time we should be caught up to meet the Lord, in the air, as He returns for His own. How would we employ the intervening days and weeks? Quite recently one of our national daily papers offered a prize for the best reply to the question: "How would you spend your last week on earth?" The question was occasioned by a businessman's false and foolish prediction that the Lord would be here on 12 June 1983.

The result of my meditation is the present message.

Several Bible saints who knew of their departure, almost to the hour, flashed across my mind. There is Moses, who, after being told of the lonely grave he would fill upon Mount Nebo, prayed, as he thought of his remaining days among the people: "Lord teach me to number my days"! There is Paul, who, if legend be true, died by the hand of an executioner and knew, just as a murderer knows, the exact hour when his spirit would be dismissed. Yet with calm confidence Paul faced eternity, saying, "I am now ready to be offered." There is our Lord Jesus, who knew that His hour had come, and who, with the shadow of Calvary over His heart, could pray, ". . . Father, the hour is come; glorify thy Son, that thy Son also may glorify thee" (John 17:1).

Why, it is an inspiration to turn to the Bible and read over the experiences of those, who, from the Great Physician, received their summonses to depart this life! See how they filled up the little while between the reception of the solemn verdict of death and its execution. It is an inspiration that should lead you to, "Go thou and do likewise!"

Three months to live! Here are some things I would strive to do, if I knew that I had only such a short period on earth, before passing the way of all flesh or being caught up to meet my Lord.

I Would Examine My Heart Life. Such an examination is necessary in order to ascertain whether I am ready to go hence—whether I am absolutely right with God. It is the height of folly to face such a near exit without being prepared for eternity.

The writer of the letter I have quoted meant to put his affairs in order before passing out into the Great Unknown. We trust this included his affairs Godward, as well as manward and that his last three months on earth—unless he encountered one of nature's miracles—brought to him the absolute certainty of sins forgiven and of a heart made ready for the other side. Then eternity would have brought him, not to the Great Unknown, but to the Great Known, even the Father's house, with its many mansions.

King Hezekiah, you will remember, received a verdict similar to the one that came to this young man. Said the Prophet Isaiah to him: ". . . Thus saith the Lord, Set thine house in order; for thou shalt die, and not live" (2 Kings 20:1).

How did Hezekiah receive this ultimatum? He turned his face to the wall and prayed. Happily for him, the fulfillment of the decree was held in abeyance for fifteen years—not by a miracle of nature, but by the will of God. My friend, if you knew all you had was three months to live, could you say that all your spiritual affairs are in order—that Jesus has already entered the disorder and confusion caused by sin and has made you ready for your translation? Do not forget that you may have only three months to live; or it may be only three weeks, three days, or three minutes. No one has any lease on life. The present moment is the only one we can claim.

Although you have not sought the advice of a physician, you might be as doomed to die as this man of forty. It has been said that we all carry about with us the seeds of trouble that will bring about our deaths. Canon Liddon, in one of his remarkable sermons, said: "Already, it may be the strongest man in this cathedral carries within himself the secret, unsuspected mischief, that will in time display itself as fatal disease, and will lay him in his grave."

That oft-recurring headache may be the tapping that will give a final blow to your brain, thus giving you a hurried dispatch into eternity. That continual cough may be nature's red signal of the coming danger of closed-up lungs and loss of breath. That persistent, gnawing pain may be the warning of a foul disease that, like the arms of an octopus, will increase its grip, until death releases you. That high blood pressure, those swollen veins, may be the forerunners of that day not far distant, when the silver cord will be loosed, the golden bowl or the pitcher will be broken at the fountain, or the wheel will be broken at the cistern—which is Solomon's descriptive way of stating those most common complaints known as heart failure and the bursting of blood vessels.

The question is—whether death comes suddenly or after a protracted illness, naturally or tragically, soon or late—are you ready to meet God? If not, then, ere pain and disease deaden your consciousness, get right with Him by accepting Jesus as your own, personal Saviour. If the Master should return in three months' time, would you be ready to meet Him?

I Would Examine My Personal Life. If, with only three months to live, death or the coming of the Lord presents no terrors—seeing that I have the assurance of a soul saved from sin and hell through the blood of the Lamb—then, I should feel it incumbent upon me to examine every part of my personal life, in order to discover how I could amend my ways.

I WOULD THINK OF HABITS I COULD CAST OFF. Habits that waste time and money, that are useless, without nobility, and harmful to the body, as well as dishonoring to the Lord, would be put in the place of death. I would make these three months the greatest period of sanctification I had ever experienced.

I WOULD THINK OF THE DEBTS I SHOULD SETTLE. It brings dishonor upon the cause of Christ when a Christian dies leaving behind debts either to be canceled by creditors or paid by friends. Beloved, because we may die or vanish at any moment, let us strive to have our affairs in order, thus leaving behind a good testimony.

I WOULD THINK OF THE ESTRANGEMENTS I SHOULD REPAIR. *Three months to live!* Then let me seek out those who have wronged me or whom I have grieved, and I shall put things right. Have I brothers and sisters, relatives, or fellow Christians from whom I am severed, as the result of some petty quarrel? Then, while my life lasts, let me exhibit the forgiving spirit of Calvary. I may die or rise to meet my Lord tomorrow. What then? Let me not delay to write the letter or speak the word that will heal the breach.

I WOULD THINK OF THE SUNSHINE I COULD SCATTER. This man of forty years, with only three months to live, tells us that in this span he means to extract more pleasure out of life by doing those things he can to help others. I would follow this example. I would examine my bankbook. After knowing that I had made the best provision for my loved ones (which of course is my first duty, according to Scripture: "But if any provide not for his own, and specially for those of his own house, he hath denied the faith, and is worse than an infidel" [1 Timothy 5:8]), I would think of all that I could do, in three months, to bring blessing to a few poor, needy souls. For if I had to see my Lord in such a time, it would please His heart to know that I had sought to change my spare gold into the current coin of loving thought and kindness.

I could not allow greed to characterize my remaining days. If I take a greedy, miserly heart to heaven with me, I shall want to snatch the gold off its shining streets, as it would pain me to see it under my feet.

I Would Examine My Christian Life. If I am a Christian as the result of a definite transaction uniting me to Christ, if accepted in the Beloved and thereby justified freely from all things, even such a stupendous work of grace does not nullify my physical dissolution. If Christ tarries, I have to die, even as the worst sinner upon earth has to die.

Being a Christian does not absolve me from death, unless, of course, my Lord returns for me by way of the air. Therefore, if, as a Christian, I have only three months to live, let me determine to get the utmost out of my spiritual privileges. Let me redeem the time by filling up the passing hours with service bearing the stamp of the divine.

I Would Make My Life More Prayerful and Holy.   Three months to live! Then let me live them in the presence of God, agonizing for the deepening of my own spiritual life and for the development of the Master's image in all my days.

Let me die to all self-pleasing, self-thought, and self-satisfaction, seeking a life radiant with the glory of my Lord. Let me live so close to heaven that a breath would waft me there.

I Would Be Active, Virile, and Self-sacrificing in His Cause.   Numbering my days, I would apply my heart unto heavenly wisdom, even unto the wisdom of winning souls. Loved ones are still unsaved: children, parents, relations, and friends are still outside the fold. My lips will soon be silent! The grave or my translation will close my testimony! Therefore, let me rescue the perishing and care for the dying, by warning them, with tears, to seek the Lord while He may be found.

I WOULD BE OBEDIENT TO HIS EVERY COMMAND.   If the time of my departure is at hand, I would endeavor to fulfill every command the Saviour enforces. He told me to eat the bread and drink the wine, as an act of loving remembrance, until He comes. Well, if He is coming for me by way of the grave or via the clouds, let me grasp every convenient opportunity of sitting at His table, thus remembering His dying love.

He, the loving, sinless Lord, went down into Jordan's waters and left me an example that I should follow His steps. Have I submitted myself to the waters of baptism as a symbol of identification with Him in death, burial, and resurrection? Then let me not forget the significance of such a holy rite. Have I not obeyed and followed my Lord thus? Then let me not hesitate to obey, as I do not want to meet the baptized Christ with disobedience upon my heart.

Through His servant Paul, He commands me to be filled with the Spirit. Only three months to live! Then, well might I pray: "Oh, Lord! May they be months of Pentecostal fullness, when out of me there shall flow rivers of living water."

I WOULD SEEK TO LIVE CALMLY AND SWEETLY FOR GOD, AMID THE DUTIES AND OBLIGATIONS OF LIFE.   Our friend who received the physician's ultimatum regarding the length of his sojourn here, remarked, "I shall carry on with my work just as I have done." What a noble resolution! And such a courageous spirit must have enabled him to die well.

Something of this same devotion is found in John Wesley's life. A lady once asked him, "Supposing that you knew that you were to die at twelve o'clock tomorrow night, how would you spend the intervening time?"

"How, madam!" he replied. "Why, just as I intend to spend it now. I should preach this evening at Gloucester and again at five tomorrow morning; after that I should ride to Tewkesbury, preach in the afternoon, and meet the societies in the evening. I should then repair to friend Martin's house, who expects to entertain me, converse and pray with the family, as usual, retire to my room at ten o'clock, commend myself to my heavenly Father, lie down to rest, and wake up in glory."

Friends, we may have less than three months to live. But, whether the period be short or long, let us not moan or despair, especially if we have any intuition regarding our end. Let us face the duties and obligations at home, the difficulties and cares of business, the monotonous tasks of our daily toil with brave, believing hearts.

If we are saved by grace, all is well! For when our last nights come, we can lay ourselves down upon our beds for a peaceful sleep and wake up in the land where the roses never fade, where there is no disease and no death.

4
Death: A Beginning or End?

In these days, when death so freely rides the winds of the world, I deem it necessary to approach such a never-worn-out subject from further, different angles. Thomas Carlyle (1795–1881), who is still acknowledged as one of the greatest writers of the Victorian age, could write feelingly of Christianity. Yet this renowned British historian, when he came to die, left this note of despair: "I am a sad old man gaping into a final chasm."

Such a sorrowful, hopeless confession compels us to ask the question, "Is death a beginning or an end?" As I am to show, it is both a conclusion and a continuation. First of all, death is an end, and there are those who believe that it is the absolute termination of a person, in respect to soul as well as to body: the "final chasm," as Carlyle expressed it, of one in his entirety.

One fears that the evolutionary theory has produced the tendency to think of man as a self-evolved, self-sustaining being: a highly evolved animal, who, when he dies, molders into dust and exists no more. Homer, the ancient Greek epic poet, expresses this view in his pathetic illustration of the leaves fading and falling in the autumn, as they are swept away by the winter winds. Thus we have the agnostic cry:

To thy dark chamber, Mother Earth, I come;
Prepare my dreamless bed for my last home;
Shut down the marble door
And leave me; let me sleep;
Never to waken more.

We are of all men most miserable, if the grave is to be our last home. There is no solace here for those with a heart hunger and a ceaseless longing for a far more blissful existence beyond the seeming catastrophe of the grave. But as I shall indicate, the consistent witness of Scripture is that the death of the body does not include the death of the individual spirit. The question of the ages is: "If a man die, shall he live again? . . ." (Job 14:14). And the Bible's own answer to such a pertinent question is: ". . . we know that if our earthly house of this tabernacle were dissolved, we have a building of God, an house not made with hands, eternal in the heavens" (2 Corinthians 5:1).

Death, then, is the end of the physical life, when the body ceases to function as the abode and expression of the life within. ". . . the body without the spirit is dead . . ." (James 2:26). No matter how hard we may strive to produce an antideath bias, sooner or later, death knocks at our doors. Half a century or so ago, it was more common for people to die in their homes. But the hospital has come to substitute for the home, and today more people die in hospitals and institutions than in homes. And death, as an end of life here below, can overtake us in several ways. Solomon would have us know that "Better is the end of a thing than the beginning thereof . . ." (Ecclesiastes 7:8). No matter how a person may die, his death is better than his birth, in that the sorrows and trials of life are over.

Many Paths to Death

Seneca said that a thousand approaches lie open to death, and observation proves that the end may come in different forms, seeing that the modes of death are manifold. It would seem as if the majority of persons die in a coma, and advancing medical science may yet make such a painless end universal. Others die in full possession of their faculties, clear and conscious until the last breath is taken. It was so with Moses, who was 120 years of age when he died, and when the end came ". . . his eye was not dim, nor his natural force abated" (Deuteronomy 34:7). The unique feature of his death is that the Lord buried him, and no man knew of his sepulchre. Moses is the only man in all history who had God as his undertaker (Deuteronomy 34:5–7). There is nothing more admirable than the victorious death of a saint, as he leaves time for eternity. When Jacob ended his death-bed instructions, we read that, ". . . he gathered up his feet into the bed, and yielded up the ghost . . ." (Genesis 49:33). What a pleasant way to end one's pilgrimage!

Apart from many who die of a disease, such as cancer or consumption, among other styles of death is that of ending one's own life. In these days of drug addiction and nerve-racking problems, suicide, as a way out of all trouble, registers an alarming increase. This was the way Judas died when, conscience stricken over his dastardly betrayal of Jesus, the renegade disciple went out and hanged himself (Matthew 27:3–8).

With no thought of death in mind, there are those who reach their ends by sudden, accidental death—a form of death all too common in these days of the motorcar and our highly mechanized industrial world. Absalom, the unworthy son King David loved, did not realize, when he fled from his father, that his mule ride would be his death ride. His head became entangled in a tree, and there he hanged, until Joab ended his misery (2 Samuel 18:9–15).

Another avenue to death is a lack of food to nourish the body. Hunger and starvation have claimed the lives of multitudes, through the ages. The children of Israel chided Moses and Aaron for having brought them from the fleshpots of Egypt to die of hunger in the wilderness (Exodus 16:3). We are daily reminded of the poverty-stricken who die from want of food; we hear of those in famine areas and refugees, reduced to skeletons, who perish from starvation. What a gruesome end this must be for those who suffer thus!

Murder and killings, all too frequent in these days when life is held cheap, are responsible for the sudden and untimely end of a vast number of people. The first recorded death of the human race was one of murder. For out of jealousy, Cain slew his brother Abel (Genesis 4:8). Peter exposed those who killed Jesus, the Prince of Life (Acts 3:15). Then think of the enormous multitudes who have been killed as the result of devastating wars. How precious is the prediction, ". . . neither shall they learn war any more" (Micah 4:3).

How can one fail to be aware of the Bible's catastrophes, such as the drowning of the human race—apart from eight souls—in the days of Noah, and the death of the great Egyptian host, who found a watery grave in the Red Sea? Likewise there were disastrous earthquakes; these biblical and historical accounts represent feared modes of death. What a tragic death Lot's wife had—as tragic as the end overtaking the Sodom she was loath to leave! For looking back at the doomed city, she became a pillar of salt (Genesis 19:26).

What must be made clear is the fact that death, no matter how it may come, is the absolute end of any further association of the dead with the world they left. Scripture makes it clear that the pre-Rapture days will witness increased satanic activity—principally along the lines of deception. Knowing that his time is short, Satan is manifesting himself, more than ever, as the deceiver. One evidence of his power to deceive even the elect can be traced to the morbid fascination of many with maintaining contact with dead relatives. Prominence has been recently focused on the stories of those who have returned from death and who renewed association with bereaved loved ones from earth.

To believe that the dead are free to roam as spirits and communicate superior spiritual wisdom to the living is a characteristic feature of demonic deception. With previous knowledge of the dead, Satan is well able to impersonate them and thereby heartlessly deceive sorrowing loved ones, as he does in the cult of Spiritualism. The unequivocal witness of Scripture is that, once dead, all who have died have no further contact with the living. Those who die without Christ as their Saviour go immediately to hell and are perpetually confined therein, until it is cast into the Lake of Fire (Revelation 20:14). As for those who die and have been saved by divine grace, the moment they are absent from their bodies, they are present with the Lord, nevermore to roam about at will. Our Lord's parable of the rich man and Lazarus is conclusive on this matter: ". . . If they [the living] hear not Moses and the prophets, neither will they be persuaded, though one rose from the dead" (Luke 16:31).

For the believer, death is the end of many aspects of life he esteemed most precious: namely, the end of his daily hours of prayer and Bible meditation; the end of his service, among men, for the Master, particularly in the area of soul winning; the end of his spiritual and secular activities; the end of his much loved relationships; the end of his earthly joys and sorrows. As he awaits the end of these things, he must ". . . be . . . sober, and watch unto prayer. . . . and hope to the end for the grace that is to be brought unto him at the revelation of Jesus Christ" (*see* 1 Peter 4:7; 1:13). It matters not how one's end may come—whether naturally or tragically, sudden or otherwise—if ours is the glorious hope that death is but the opening of a gate into a larger and more blessed life. For all such, death has no terrors, but comes as a welcome friend, bidding us to enter the ivory palaces above. Paul Gerhardt has taught us to sing:

Let us in life and death
Thy steadfast truth declare,
And publish with our latest breath
Thy love and guardian care.

Death: A Beginning

Having considered all that is involved in death as an end,
let us now think of it as a beginning. A word is necessary
regarding the finality of death. For instance, the Psalmist
says, "For in death there is no remembrance of thee: in the
grave who shall give thee thanks?" and, "The dead praise
not the Lord, neither any that go down into silence" (Psalms
6:5; 115:17). Solomon expresses a similar thought in the
phrase, ". . . the dead know not any thing. . ." (Ecclesiastes
9:5). The implication of these verses is apparent: Corpses
can neither think, sing, nor talk. Those, however, who lived
in those dead bodies continue to have life and consciousness, or a beginning, in another world.

While, as I have already pointed out, death is likened
unto sleep and is only associated with the body, the Lord
does not arouse you from the final sleep; for the soul—you,
yourself—does not enter into an unconscious state at death,
but immediately travels into a chosen destiny beyond
death. This is why, for the Christian, ". . . the day of death is
better than the day of one's birth" (*see* Ecclesiastes 7:1). The
sunset of death passes into the sunrise of glory. John Milton, one of England's greatest poets, gave utterance to the
worth of death as he faced the end of his God-honoring life:
"That Golden Key that opes the Palace of Eternity." As he
neared his end, John Newton exclaimed, "I am still in the
land of the dying; I shall be in the land of the living soon."
Anna Letitia Barbauld, in extreme old age, gave us one of
the finest verses in English literature, when she wrote of
death as a beginning:

> Life! We've been long together,
> Through pleasant and through cloudy weather;
> 'Tis hard to part when friends are dear—
> Perhaps 'twill cost a sigh, a tear;
>   Then steal away; give little warning,
> Choose thine own time;
> Say not, Good Night,—But in some brighter clime,
>   Bid me, Good Morning.

Bless God, there is a nevertheless afterward! For all the redeemed, there is the beginning of a never-ending fellowship with Him who died, but is alive forevermore. Here is the beginning of a sojourn in the continuing city we have ever longed for, a place in which the sins, sorrows, and separation of earth are unknown. It is the beginning of a perfect service for the Master, as John depicts in the revelation of heaven, where His servants see His face and serve Him (Relevation 22:3).

Alas! For those who die in their sin and without Christ as their Saviour, the beginning on the other side will be one of despair and remorse—the beginning of eternal woe and torment! As soon as the rich man Jesus described came to his end, he began his eternity in hell. His cries for relief went unanswered, and his prayer—for someone to be sent to warn his unsaved relatives not to follow him into the caverns of the lost—was unheeded. How different was his end from the new beginning of Lazarus—who died with a sore-stricken body and in abject poverty, but who began his eternity in paradise, with its absence of disease and poverty. Oh, what a marvelous change for a beggar!

5

When Death Is Gain

Approaching another feature of dying and death, we recognize that belief in some manner of existence after death is a catholic belief of humanity and can be discovered in every part of the world, in every age, and among those representing every degree and variety of culture. While there are differences as to the exact nature of immortality, nevertheless, savages and civilized peoples alike hold forth belief in some aspect of a future state.

Our Lord was not the first to unfold the truth of an afterlife to the minds of men. Nowhere in the Gospels is it asserted that He taught something novel and without antecedent, in respect to man's survival beyond the grave. What is claimed for Him is that He ". . . brought life and immortality to light through the gospel" (2 Timothy 1:10). What Paul affirms in this passage is that Jesus gave lucidity to what was obscure, completeness to what was fragmentary, certainty to what was probable. And it is His clear and authoritative teaching, which the apostles imbibed, that shaped the Christian view of death and of the life to follow. It is this view I now wish to fully consider.

Facing the Gates of Death

The Psalmist could speak of the Lord as the One who lifted him up from the gates of death (Psalms 9:13). Many of the Lord's people have known what it is to arrive almost at

the gates of death, but not to die; and being restored, they
have declared the goodness and mercy of God and also how
believers should encounter death; their last enemy (Psalms
118:17). A survey of some of the apostolic declarations regarding this conquered enemy reveals the conception of the
early church as to our death and final destiny. Writing to
the believers in Rome, Paul sent the positive statement:

> ... none of us liveth to himself, and no man dieth to
> himself. For whether we live, we live unto the Lord; and
> whether we die, we die unto the Lord: whether we live
> therefore, or die, we are the Lord's. For to this end Christ
> both died, and rose, and revived, that he might be Lord
> both of the dead and living.
>
> Romans 14:7–9

Then in his magnificent resurrection chapter, the apostle
was just as explicit, when he wrote:

> ... this corruptible must put on incorruption, and this
> mortal must put on immortality. So when this corruptible
> shall have put on incorruption, and this mortal shall have
> put on immortality, then shall be brought to pass the say-
> ing that is written, Death is swallowed up in victory. O
> death, where is thy sting? O grave, where is thy victory? ...
> But thanks be to God, which giveth us the victory through
> our Lord Jesus Christ.
>
> 1 Corinthians 15:53–55, 57; *see also* 2 Corinthians 5

Such a sure and solid hope for the future gives incentive
for service in the present, and so the saints awaiting their
participation in this glorious triumph over death must be
"... stedfast, unmoveable, always abounding in the work of
the Lord ..." (1 Corinthians 15:58). In his letter to the Philippians, Paul voices the same viewpoint of believers whose
citizenship is in heaven and who await the coming of the

Saviour, "Who shall change our vile body, that it may be fashioned like unto his glorious body, according to the working whereby he is able even to subdue all things unto himself" (Philippians 3:21).

Catherine Booth, devoted and gifted wife of the founder of the Salvation Army, had the Spirit-inspired approach to death, for her last words were: "The waters are rising but I am not sinking. Do not be concerned about dying. Go on living well; the dying will be right." The proverb has it, "Truth sits upon the lips of a dying man." This was certainly true in the final utterance of Mrs. Booth.

To Die Is Gain

So far, in these meditations, I have had much to say about death as the inescapable event overtaking all men and as the final exit from a sin-stricken world. But to Paul, death was not a lamentable end or a tragic loss in the family circle, but a most beneficial advantage to those who can read their title clear to mansions in the sky. Although a prisoner at the time, Paul could send a joyful letter to the Philippians and affirm, "For me to live is Christ, and to die is gain" and that he was ". . . in a strait betwixt two, having a desire to depart, and to be with Christ; which is far better" (Philippians 1:21, 23).

". . . To die is gain," ". . . to be with Christ; which is far better." How these assuring phrases lift death out of all its morbidity and clothe it with the garment of profitable acquisition! At death, we are forced to surrender all material advantages and possessions, but the eternal gains are tremendous. For Paul, who saw Christ on that Damascus road, knew what it was to have Him as the One in whom he lived, moved, and had his being. Christ was the center and circumference of his entire life; wherein was there a greater advantage in dying? Was it not in being in a personal and eternal fellowship with the Christ he loved, lived, and died for—without the limitations and frustrations of this earthly life? Paul shared the confident hope of Job: ". . . mine eyes shall behold [him], and not another . . ." (19:27).

Presently, Christ is "the King . . . invisible . . . ," and we endure as those who have seen Him who is invisible (1 Timothy 1:17; Hebrews 11:27). Peter commended the saints for their walk by faith, with the words: "Whom having not seen, ye love; in whom, though now ye see him not, yet believing, ye rejoice with joy unspeakable and full of glory" (1 Peter 1:8). "Believing is seeing." This is why we sing with Ray Palmer:

> Jesus, these eyes have never seen
> That radiant form of Thine;
> The veil of sense hangs dark between
> Thy blessed face and mine.

But our death will bring the glorious gain of seeing Him, the King of Glory, in all His majesty and splendor. The affirmation of John—the disciple Jesus loved, and the one who often gazed upon the human face of the Master, and who closed the Revelation of Him as the glorified, all-conquering One—is most emphatic: "They shall see his face; and his name shall be in their foreheads" (Revelation 22:4). As we linger amid the shadows, awaiting the end bringing us face-to-face with our Redeemer, we can clasp the hope of David to our hearts and make it our own, "As for me, I will behold thy face in righteousness: I shall be satisfied, when I awake, with thy likeness" (Psalms 17:15). Death's advantage in such a transformation is likewise expressed by John: ". . . we shall be like him; for we shall see him as he is" (1 John 3:2).

As He is! What an arrestive phrase this is. How is He? What is His composition? Well, He is exactly as He was on His ascension day, when He was taken up into heaven with the, human, glorified body He rose with from the grave. This is one of the marvels of heaven: Some of humanity's dust, glorified, seated on a throne. And, when we see Him, we shall be like Him. The mortal will have put on immortality and the corruptible, the incorruptible. From the dust there will blossom red life that shall be endless.

Then we have the further Pauline pronouncement, "... to depart, and to be with Christ ... is far better." Far better than what? In the narrative, Paul speaks of his quandry of making a choice between two spheres: whether he should remain on the earth and continue caring for the spiritual life of the Philippians or whether to go to heaven and be with Christ, which would have been the better choice. Paul, however, chose to abide in the flesh, which was more needful for the saints at Philippi (Philippians 1:22–26). To be with Christ in heaven is better in every way than the best we have below—even our service for the Master, which is often marred by self-dependence and self-glory. Describing the heavenly abode, John says, "... his servants shall serve Him" (Revelation 22:3), and service there will be far better than any we could render Him on earth.

At the death of his wife, Robert Browning penned the following citation from the poet Dante in her much-loved testament:

> Thus I believe, thus I affirm, thus I am certain it is
> that from this life I shall pass to another better, there
> that lady lives, of whom my soul is enamoured.

For believers, however, what makes the Glory land the better country that the saints of old sighed for is the presence of Him who is alive forevermore—the One whom, in our hearts, do we love (Hebrews 11:15, 16). John Dryden would have us remember that:

> Like pilgrims to th' appointed place we tend;
> The world's an inn, and death the journey's end.

But while death is a welcome end, it is also the glorious beginning of a better journey into another place that the deathless One is preparing for us, where God's love and justice are resplendent in our eternal acquittal and where they will be eternally honored in our endless salvation. He it was who drew the plan of our redemption, sent His Son to execute the plan, and imparted His Holy Spirit to bring us into the realization of such a plan. At last He will receive us to Himself, of purest grace. "I give unto them eternal life," says the Saviour, "and they shall never perish . . ." (John 10:28).

Meantime, though our hearts may be strong and brave, they, "like muffled drums, are beating Funeral marches to the grave," as Henry Wadsworth Longfellow expresses it. Scripture emphasizes what manner of persons we ought to be. We should be found unconcerned with things of earth and aiming at things eternal. We ought to be holy, prayerful, patient, and expectant. Contented with such things as we have, we should die daily, to be rich in good works, laying up for ourselves treasures in heaven. Paul could confess that what things were gain to him, he counted loss for Christ (Philippians 3:7). If we believe that we are able to be like Jesus, when we see Him as He is, then John reminds us, ". . . every man that hath this hope in him purifieth himself, even as Jesus is pure" (1 John 3:3).

Yours is the privilege of waiting upon the dying, warning them of the tragedy of coming to the end without the assurance of salvation; or, if they are the Lord's, you may comfort them at their departing, emulating the example of Richard Baxter:

> I preached as never sure to preach again,
> And as a dying man to dying men.

For each of us, as we linger amid the shadows and see through a glass darkly, may "the Lord direct our hearts into his love, and into the patient waiting for Christ" (*see* 2 Thessalonians 3:5). Let us gladly await the Lord's call, "Come up hither"; silently submit ourselves to His will; and acknowledge His right to conceal the cause of His working, until He has perfectly accomplished His designs. Since our bodies return to the dust from which they came, may we be found presenting them to the Lord as living sacrifices, so that out of them rivers of living water may flow, refreshing the arid wilderness around. It is only thus that we will be ready to sing, as Henry F. Lyte has taught us to do:

> Hold Thou Thy Cross before my closing eyes;
> Shine through the gloom, and point me to the skies;
> Heaven's morning breaks, and earth's vain shadows flee;
> In life, in death, O Lord, abide with me.

6

The Auction of Souls

"I am my beloved's, and his desire is toward me" (Song of Solomon 7:10). ". . . Satan hath desired to have you . . ." (Luke 22:31). The combination of these passages expresses the deep, solemn truth concerning rival bidders for the soul of man. One bidder is heavenly, the other hellish; one sacred, the other satanic; one fair, the other foul; one beautiful, the other bestial; one blesses, the other blasts; one is the Reigning Lord, the other a raging lion.

The conflict for the mastery of a human life greatly resembles an auction room, with its eagerness among bidders to secure some of the priceless goods offered. No two bidders can secure the same article, seeing that it is knocked down to the highest bidder. With such a figure before our minds, let us apply it to the battle for the possession of precious souls.

First of all, we have the auction room, which is the inner life—the hidden room of the heart. Then come the rival bidders, the Saviour and Satan, the Lord and the liar. The treasures for auction are the possessions of one's whole being. The auctioneer who disposes of his wares is the will of man, which is the deciding factor in matters relating to the soul.

The Auction Room

Such a room is both seen and unseen. It is within your heart and also in your room, as you ponder this message, or in a church as you listen to the Gospel being preached. When you enter God's House, great issues confront you. Rivals are there, earnestly desiring to have you. Holy voices urge you to repent; hellish influences constrain you to reject the Saviour.

The auction market is also within your heart. Man's innermost being is ever the ultimate battlefield. The Saviour, with eyes of love, heart of compassion, and hands of mercy, stands before the soul and, with the wooing notes of grace, strikes to win the allegiance He truly deserves. Satan, with his devilish hatred, diabolical purpose, and hands stained with the blood of multitudes both in and out of hell, likewise waits to clutch the sinner, who, understanding the claims of these rival bidders, must knock down his soul to one of them.

The Rival Bidders

This message may help a perplexed soul to a right decision, if it can suggest the opposite characters of the Saviour and Satan: one a friend, the other a foe. The devil brings a curse, the Master a blessing; one darkness, the other light; one death, the other life; one is from hell, the other from heaven.

The above passages have a direct application to the saint, for within him there is the constant struggle for mastery. Satan, of course, is cognizant of the fact that he cannot repossess a saved person, but he can cripple the Christian's testimony. The enemy desired to have Job (Job 1:6–12). God said, "My desire is that Job may be tried unto the end . . ." (Job 34:36). And until our end, Christ and Satan will ever be in conflict over the mastery of our lives. The devil will take advantage of his permission to tempt us. By subtle devices, he will endeavor to wreck our witness and send us to heaven maimed. It was thus that he desired to have Peter. ". . . Satan hath desired to have you . . ." (Luke 22:31). There the word *desire* means "to ask exclusively for" or "to practically demand." Christ's intercession on Peter's behalf prevailed, however, over the enemy's purpose.

And let us make no mistake about the fact that Satan desires to have the saint—that is, to ruin his spirituality or to keep him out of the realization of the fullness of the blessing of God. Christ, on the other hand, yearns for and strives after the believer's sanctification. As the King of saints, He greatly desires their beauty (Psalms 45:11).

The sinner must know the character of the rival bidders for his soul, ere he hands over such a treasure to one of them.

Look for a Moment at the Contrast of the Bidders' Names: Let us take Satan. Who is he? How does the Bible describe him?

He is the serpent: subtle, cunning, unsuspected in his approach.

He is the adversary: that is, the antagonist of God and man.

He is the devil, a name meaning "to throw down."

He is a murderer and, as such, is responsible for wars, murders, and suicides.

He is a liar, a deceiver. Falsity is his stock-in-trade.

He is the prince of demons, and he marshals all evil forces for your destruction.

He is the roaring lion: devouring, savage, out to consume.

He is Apollyon: a destroyer of all that is good and fair.

He is the dragon: bestial, hateful, fierce.

He is an angel of light: plausible, gilding his hollow pleasures.

Oh, how can man be content to follow and serve this hound of hell? He has no good intentions for any soul.

Let us take the Saviour! Is He different? What is He like?

He is the One who created us all and who loves us with an undying love!

He is the Beloved, the Shepherd, the Friend, the Fairest Among Ten Thousand.

His name is as ointment poured forth.
He is the Way, the Truth, and the Life.
He was the Lamb dying for the sins of the world.

Can it be that you see no beauty in Him? Does He have no form or comeliness for you? Are you blinded by sin and prejudice, so that He is only as a root out of dry ground to you? Does His name not thrill your soul? Has His Word no charm for you?

Consider, in the Next Place, the Contrast of Their Histories!   What is the record of Satan? Why, it is as black as his character! He it was who created sorrow among the angels. He was responsible for the entrance of sin; the murder of Abel; the desolation of the Flood; and for the tears, graves, sins, sobs, and miseries of mankind down all the ages. The darkness and terrible sins of heathenism, the appalling, iniquitous practices all around, the cesspool of evil within the heart of man are all the products of Satan's wicked mind. Yet when this fiend presses his claims, multitudes hand over the precious possession of life—without a thought! What folly!

Has the Saviour a different testimony? Can we safely trust our souls to His care? What is His record? Scripture reveals Him as the loving and obedient One, loving and loved by all who appreciate His worth (Proverbs 8:30, 31). As the Creator and Sustainer of everything that lives, He bountifully supplies all necessary meat in due season. Condescending, sympathizing, suffering was He as He lived among men. His passion to save men led Him to be crucified in cold blood. He ever yearned over souls, that life eternal might be theirs. He never thought a wrong thought, uttered a wrong word, or committed a wrong action. None could convict Him of sin. He was holy, harmless, undefiled, separate from sinners, higher than the highest, better than the best. O what a Saviour! And yet so many treat Him with contempt and slam the door of mercy in the face of this best Friend a sinner could possibly have.

There Is the Contrast of Their Purposes! What motives actuate these bidders as they strive for the supremacy over the hearts of men? Is there any conflict in their desires?

TAKE SATAN! Is he inspired by good intentions, as he approaches man? Good intentions! Why, he is just as much a stranger to them as he is to the truth! He is out for the delusion of the soul, for its loss now and its damnation hereafter. His heart—if he has one—is filled with a dual diabolical purpose: to blast souls and to have them in the Lake of Fire eternally. Knowing that he is without hope, he labors incessantly to people hell with the Christ-less. Ever before him is the destruction of the work of the Trinity on behalf of a sinning world. And what a mystery it is that so many sin-driven lives blindly follow such a cruel monarch!

TAKE JESUS! What are His thoughts toward us as He stands and pleads: "Come unto me"? Is it peace, as He urges us to join Him in His chariot? His desire to help us can be proved by the fact that He was manifested that He might destroy the works of the devil for all sinning souls. And now, unwearyingly, He labors to deliver men from the penalty and tyranny of sin. He seeks the ennoblement of life, the enrichment of it by the importation of His own fragrant life. He offers weary hearts present rest and eternal bliss. Our good is ever His wish. But can you understand it? Many there are who are yet content to feed on ashes or the husks the swine do eat, rather than on the bread of the Father's house. Thrice happy are the souls who can say, "O Christ, Thou art my supreme joy! Thy blessed will and mine are one. I have no desires but Thine, no pleasures but such as please Thy happy heart."

The Treasures for Auction

What are the goods exposed for sale? Are the lots for disposal somewhat rare and costly? The truth is that no auctioneer's catalogue or market ever contained such valuable treasures—for did not Jesus declare that one soul is worth more than all the world contains?

The treasures are the whole being, time, talents, possessions, influence, and eternal destiny of a soul. And all that it is and has must go to one bidder or the other. Both Christ and Satan appraise the worth of a soul; hence they struggle in different ways for its possession.

> To lose one's wealth is much
> To lose one's health is more
> To lose one's soul is such a loss that nothing can restore.

As we realize the truth of these words, what wisdom we manifest when we permit the Saviour to save the soul and have it in His eternal care.

The Auctioneer

With such costly possessions before the bidders, surely the auctioneer must be weighted with the sense of responsibility for their right disposal. Pearls of greatest price must not be thrown away for a pittance. Who, then, is the auctioneer? He is your will, for upon the human will rests the solemn responsibility for who shall have the soul. The will listens to the bids and then makes its choice. Cried Pilate when Christ and Barabbas were on his hands, ". . . Whether of the twain will ye that I release unto you? . . ." (Matthew 27:21). And your will is your Pilate making a choice between Christ and Satan. Pilate, we read, released unto them him whom they desired. The fatal choice that day was for Barabbas. On the other hand, we have the record of those who desired to see Jesus (Luke 23:25; John 12:21). The Jews desired Barabbas! The Greeks desired Jesus! Whom have you chosen? Who has your allegiance? Can you truthfully confess, "Whom have I in heaven but thee? and there is

none upon earth that I desire beside Thee"? (Psalms 73:25).
Your will is ever the deciding factor as to whom is to be the
master of your life.

The well-known story of Rowland Hill and his experience at an open-air service will stand repetition. As he
preached the Gospel, a lady rode by; and, as Rowland Hill
glanced at her, he noticed that she was bedecked with
jewels and was quite content, as she nestled in the corner of
her coach. The truth she heard from earnest lips that day
has been cast in the following form, by an unknown poet:

THE THREE BIDDERS

Will you listen, friends, for a moment
    While a story I unfold;
A marvelous tale of a wonderful sale
    of a noble lady of old;
How hand and heart at an auction mart,
    Soul and body she has sold.

And now in His Name a sale I proclaim,
And bids for this fair lady call.
Who will purchase the whole—her body and soul
    Coronet, jewels, and all?

I see already three Bidders—
The World steps up as the first.
"I will give her my treasures, and all the pleasures
    For which my votaries thirst.
She shall dance each day, more joyous and gay
    With a quiet grave at the worst."

But out speaks the Devil boldly;
    "The kingdoms of earth are mine.
Fair lady, thy name with an envied fame
    On their brightest tablets shall shine.
Only give me thy soul and I give thee the whole
    Their glory and wealth to be thine."

And pray, what hast Thou to offer,
Thou Man of Sorrows unknown?
    And He gently said, "My blood I have shed,
To purchase her for mine own.
To conquer the grave, and her soul to save
    I trod the winepress alone.
I will give her My cross of suffering
    My cup of sorrow to share,
But with endless love, in My Home above,
    All shall be righted there.
She shall walk in the light, in a robe of white,
    And a radiant crown shall wear."

Thou hast heard the terms, fair lady,
    That each hath offered for thee.
Which wilt thou choose, and which wilt thou lose
    This life, or the life to be?
The fable was mine, but the choice is thine,
    Sweet lady, which of the three?

She took from her hands the jewels,
    The coronet from her brow.
"Lord Jesus," she said, as she bowed her head,
    "The highest bidder art Thou.
Thou gav'st for my sake Thy life, and I take
    Thy offer—and take it now.
I know the world and her pleasures
    At best they weary and cloy;
And the tempter is bold, but his houses and gold
    Prove ever a fatal decoy.
I long for Thy rest—Thy bid is the best,
    Lord, I accept it with joy."

Believing then, that Christ's bid is the best, may we ever
receive it with joy.

7
Death and Destiny

In this meditation revolving around the solemn theme of dying and death, we have reached a consideration of the question regarding whether or not there is any destiny after death. Does death end all? Is it a terminal or a leap in the dark? When we die, are we done altogether, or do we live again in another realm? Job inquired, "If a man die, shall he live again? . . ." (14:14). Is there any existence beyond the grave? Or when we die, are we—like animals and birds—completely extinguished? If not, where are the dead?

Scripture's authentic voice affirms that, although physical death is the evidence and result of sin, as a terminal, it only affects the body. There is no cessation of life and consciousness after death, as Jesus' parable of the rich man and Lazarus clearly proves (Luke 16:19–31). Further, could any statement be more explicit regarding the continuity of life after death than that by the writer of Hebrews: ". . . it is appointed unto men once to die, *but after this* the judgment"? (9:27, *italics mine*). To this witness of an afterlife, we can add the declaration of Paul: "If in this life *only* we have hope in Christ, we are of all men most miserable" (1 Corinthians 15:19, *italics mine*). The apostle also says that death is not oblivion, but is swallowed in victory (1 Corinthians 15:54; *see also* Isaiah 25:8). Hosea was not less confident of the continuance of life beyond death, when he wrote, ". . . we shall live in his sight" (6:2).

Heaven or Hell?

The Psalmist would have us remember that "... unto
God the Lord belong the issues from death" (Psalms 68:20).
Twice over in this psalm the Lord describes Himself as the
God of salvation (Psalms 68:19, 20), but this is how He
functions *only* up to the hour of death, for there is no salvation after death. Where are the dead, then? Why, where
they decided to go before they died. The predetermined
issues of death, David mentions, are of a two-fold nature:
namely, the issue of heaven for those who have God as their
salvation and hell for those who die in their sins (John
14:1–4; Luke 16:19–31). Eternal bliss versus eternal woe is
the issue to be faced as we leave this present world.

The Bible offers humanity no purgatory. There is no in-
termediate state after death, where the departed can remain
until they have atoned for their sins committed on earth and
where, through a purifying process, their actions can elimi-
nate the fearful prospect of eternal anguish and prepare
themselves for everlasting peace. Accept the inevitable fact
that, if the Lord does not return in your lifetime, the day is
marked on God's calendar when you must look death in the
face. There will be a spot where your dust will find its natural abode and where the world's ambition, the strife of
tongues, and the conflict of passions will float past but as
night winds sighing over a deserted shrine. We are guilty of
gross and fatal negligence if we fail to heed the solemn
warning of Scripture, "How shall we escape, if we neglect so
great salvation ... "? (Hebrews 2:3).

There is no uncertainty regarding the alternatives the soul
must choose from: "Behold, I set before you this day a
blessing and a curse" (Deuteronomy 11:26); "... I have set
before you life and death, blessing and cursing: therefore
choose life, that both thou and thy seed may live" (Deuteronomy 30:19); "... choose you this day whom ye will
serve ..." (Joshua 24:15); "He that believeth on the Son

hath everlasting life: and he that believeth not the Son shall not see life; but the wrath of God abideth on him" (John 3:36). In his prophecy of Christ, Isaiah says that He "shall know to refuse the evil, and choose the good ..." (Isaiah 7:15, 16). The character of life here and our destiny after death depend upon our personal choices. What a solemn obligation, then, is ours! We can choose the nature of our own eternity: heaven or hell, everlasting bliss or woe, the eternal fellowship of the heavenly host or the unending association with the devil and the myriads of lost souls. The choice confronts us until death closes the door upon the freedom to choose, and we enter the kind of eternity our human will has decided upon. Let us consider the nature of these alternatives.

Having reached this phase of our general theme, it is essential to consider the significance of the terms used. Hell, hades, and Sheol are equivalent terms, representing the abode of all the dead—whether the righteous or the wicked. Whatever term you use, this was the home of all departed souls. It was divided into two sections, as our Lord described in the narrative of the rich man and Lazarus (Luke 16:19–31).

The Upper Chamber

This section was known as Abraham's Bosom or paradise, and all who died in faith, up until Christ's ascension, entered this blessed abode (Hebrews 11:1–16; Luke 16:22; 23:43). Only two Old Testament saints never died, but were translated straight to heaven: Enoch and Elijah. At death, Jesus, along with the dying thief—the first trophy of His redemption—joined the happy fellowship of the saints in paradise (Luke 23:43). The Apostles' Creed states it "He descended into hell," meaning the portion of it where all the righteous were prisoners of hope. During His three days therein, we read that "... he ... preached unto the spirits in prison" (1 Peter 3:19).

Having "the keys of hell and of death," doubtless Jesus preached to the righteous of the eternal bliss awaiting them in His Father's immediate presence in heaven. He no doubt spoke to the unrighteous of His utmost endeavor to save them from hell, but of their rejection of His love and appeal and their consequent doom—a solemn sermon Abraham likewise preached (Luke 16:25, 26; Matthew 23:37). After His three days in this resting place of those who died in faith, Jesus rose again and remained on earth for forty days and then ascended to His Father's home in heaven (Acts 1:1–11). Paul, however, reminds us that Jesus never ascended alone, but that He led a retinue of saints with Him: ". . . When he ascended up on high, he led captivity captive. . . . ascended up far above all heavens . . ." (Ephesians 4:8, 10). Since the Ascension, paradise has been vacant and believers, when they die, go directly to heaven. They are no longer prisoners of delight and hope, in Abraham's Bosom, but, along with Abraham, citizens of the heavenly country (John 14:3; Acts 1:10, 11; 2 Corinthians 5:8). When we are absent from the body, we shall be at home with the Lord, beholding Him in all His glory and beauty. Now, for the child of God, paradise is His immediate presence.

The Lower Chamber

This underneath section is known as the pit, the bottomless pit, or hell. It is here the rich man was tormented, and it is here that all the wicked and the nations forgetting God are consigned (Psalms 9:17). "Yet thou shalt be brought down to hell, to the sides of the pit" (Isaiah 14:15). This is hell, ever enlarging itself to receive the vast number of the godless, at death (Isaiah 5:14, 15). That it was the underneath portion is evident from the posture of the rich man who lifted up his eyes and saw Abraham above. Further, between the two apartments there was a ". . . great gulf fixed. . . ," and no contact or communication was possible between the righteous and the doomed (Luke 16:26). Salvation or deliverance for these hopeless prisoners is also impossible (Luke 16:27-31). There is no purgatory in which sinners can be made fit for heaven.

The bottomless pit, as "the lower part," remains. It is the hell all the godless, past and present, are turned into and which all sinners who are still in the flesh fear and face. It is also to be the dread abode of the beast and false prophets and of Satan, who will be imprisoned within it for a thousand years (Revelation 9:1-11; 11:7; 17:8; 20:1-3). The final depository of all who die out of Christ is not hell, but the Lake of Fire, referred to as the second death. The first death was a physical termination, when the soul was separated from the body. The second death implies the eternal separation of spirit and soul from God. The present solemn task of all who are saved and delivered from the wrath to come is to warn sinners to flee from such wrath, to rescue the unsaved while the door of mercy stands ajar. Thrice blessed are they who, by grace, have been delivered ere death claims them, from the lowest hell (Psalms 86:13). Blessed are those who daily live in the assurance that, when they come to cross the bar, they will see their heavenly Pilot, face-to-face (1 Corinthians 13:9-13).

Paul Golding, an English poet who died about 1590, welcomed the next world with confidence, with these last words:

> This is Heaven! I not only feel the climate, but I breathe the ambrosial air of Heaven, and soon shall enjoy the company.

While we linger here below, we are not to be so heavenly minded as to be of no earthly use. Yet we must live and labor as pilgrims who are traveling to the Celestial City, where we shall see the King in all His beauty and delivered from all the trammeling influences of the flesh. Then we shall offer Him perfect and eternal love and service, throughout the countless ages of eternity. The Psalmist emphasized the universality of death in the words, "... wise men die, likewise the fool and the brutish person perish ..." but he also revealed that God will redeem your soul and mine from the power of the grave, as He receives us unto Himself (Psalms 49:10, 15).

Up till now I have dealt largely with the certainty, nature, and issues of death; but what we must not lose sight of is the glorious fact that, if we are the Lord's, like Enoch and Elijah, we may never taste death. Countless numbers of believers the world over may never die. With his dim vision of the Rapture of saints, the Psalmist could say, "Gather my saints together unto me; those that have made a convenant with me by sacrifice" (Psalms 50:5). The blessed hope of the Gospel is the gathering of the saints together to meet the Saviour in the air. We sometimes sing, "Oh Joy, Oh Delight! Should we go without dying." And we may not die, for Paul assured us that, when Jesus returns for His own— as He said He would—if we are alive when He appears, ours will be the joy of being caught to meet Him in the air (1 Thessalonians 4:13–18). Thus we should not so much be taken up with death as being the end of all the sins, sorrows, and separations of earth, but with its being our Lord's glorious appearing when He will receive us unto Himself. We should be looking, not for death, but for the promised Coming of Him who vanquished death, with all its power. Henry Alford would have us sing:

> Bring near Thy great salvation,
> Thou Lamb for sinners slain;
> Fill up the role of Thine elect,
> Then take Thy power and reign;
> Appear, Desire of nations,
> Thine exiles long for home;
> Show in the heaven Thy promised sign;
> Thou Prince and Saviour, come.

8

Outer Darkness

As there is a discreet silence in the majority of our pulpits—a forcing into the background of the true and awfully solemn teaching about hell—it behooves us to deal fearlessly with such a subject, keeping nothing back. Well, what saith the Scriptures? Turning to the teachings of our Lord, we find certain truths standing out in bold relief. And in dealing with what He had to say about hell, let us remind ourselves of His outstanding sympathy with suffering, His tenderness of heart and of spirit, His unselfishness in relieving all suffering.

Here are some of His words concerning hell and man's passage there:

> Jesus speaks of "the broad way that leadeth to destruction" (*see* Matthew 7:13), affirming that there are two ways, with two radically different ends.
>
> When He says ". . . depart from me, ye that work iniquity" (Matthew 7:23), our Lord indicates that religious hypocrisy now will result in banishment from His presence, in the future life.
>
> Jesus used many descriptions of hell in His parables. Matthew 8:12 says unbelievers will be ". . . cast out into outer darkness. . . ." He uses the same dread language in the parables of Matthew 22:13 and 25:30. The description of "the day of judgment" is thrice repeated in Matthew 10:15; 11:22, 24. The furnace of

fire is spoken of in Matthew 13:41, 42 and repeated,
with variation, in verses 49, 50. Nothing could be
more heartbreaking! In Mark 9:43–46 we have the
triple phrase about the undying worm and the unquenched fire. In Matthew 25:41–46 He speaks of
eternal fire and eternal punishment. John 3:36 describes the abiding wrath of God.

The impression to be gathered from the sayings of Christ
has been forcibly expressed by Professor James Salmond, in
his volume *The Christian Doctrines of Immortality*, when he
comes to deal with the absoluteness of Jesus' words: "If
there is no Hell, as He said there was, then He stands
branded as a trickster, a colossal liar."

The finality of destiny could scarcely be more unequivo-
cally expressed than it is when Christ concludes His dis-
course of judgment, with the last contrast: "And these shall
go away into everlasting punishment: but the righteous into
life eternal" (Matthew 25:46). Christ gives the last issues of
life with a notable frequency, in different forms of dis-
course—sometimes in outline, sometimes in large represen-
tation. Exclusion from the Kingdom and banishment from
Himself are the ends of those who have the language of
faith, but not its fruits (Matthew 7:21–23). Repudiation is
the sentence of those who deny Him before men (Matthew
10:33; Luke 9:26). Inability to enter the Kingdom of heaven
is the judgment of the merciless and ambitious (Matthew
18:3–35); weeping and gnashing of teeth, in the furnace of
fire, that of the selfish (Matthew 13:42). The outer darkness
is the destiny of the unprofitable (Matthew 25:30). The same
impression is conveyed by many of His words that are of
larger and more general meaning: those that speak of losing
one's soul or forfeiting one's life (Mark 8:36); of perishing (John 3:16); of dying in one's sins (John 8:21–24); of its
being good never to have been born (Matthew 26:24; Mark
14:21); those, too, in which—leaving the exclusion of

the opposite class to suggest itself—He declares eternal life to be for him who believes (John 3:15); and those in which—giving both aspects of the spiritual condition—He says of him who believes, that he "is not judged," but of him who believes not, that he "hath been judged already" (John 3:18).

Christ's own teaching, we must conclude, gives the significance of finality to the moral decisions of life. He never softens the awful responsibilities of this life, even by the dim adumbration of any change. His recorded sayings nowhere suggest the provision of ministries of grace, whether now or continued in the after existence. They nowhere speak of a place in the other world where there may be repentance unto life.

And equally final is the teaching of the apostles. Paul speaks of a day appointed, when God will judge the world (Acts 17:31; Romans 2:5–9). Peter emphasizes the judgment of the wicked and the destruction of this earth (2 Peter 2:4–3:7). Jude, in his intense little letter, tells us about the blackness of darkness (v. 6). John has some terrible things to say about the wicked in the Revelation: There is the Lake of Fire and the second death (21:8); without are dogs (22:15); each man's choice is fixed (22:11).

Now, who shall speak after God? Who shall give contrary opinions, after the Book has spoken? We have the teaching of the infallible Christ and of holy men who spoke as they were moved by the infallible, holy Christ. And their combined revelation must be the last word on the subject of hell. "And the ostrich shutting its eyes to danger became a sure victim of the danger. We'll do well not to see an ostrich if there's a mirror at hand."

The Terms Used

Words are dangerous things, if not carefully watched, owing to their tendency to change meaning as a language grows or is translated; a brief review of the words and terms used in connection with the doom of the wicked will help us to a right understanding of the subject before us.

The Words <u>Damn</u> and <u>Damnation</u>.   Although such words convey the idea of the sinner's eternal punishment, it must be borne in mind that, when used by our Lord and when translated out of the original, they did not mean what we now impute to them. They are connected with two Greek words meaning "to judge" and to judge adversely or to condemn. In the Revised Standard Version, the words *damn* and *damnation* are swept away.

The Word <u>Hell</u>.   This word occurs eighteen times in the King James Version. In five cases it is a translation of the word *hades;* twelve times it is a translation of the word *Gehenna,* used by our Lord; once it is translated from *Tartarus.* Now, although the English word *hell* has come to mean, almost exclusively, the place of torment of the wicked, that was not its original significance. *Hell* is akin to *heal,* that is, "to cover" (as a wound with skin). It was used in regard to the tiling or slating of a house, by which act it was covered in. And the meaning "the covered, the hidden region," expresses the Hebrew *Sheol* and the Greek *hades:* the covered state of all, both good and bad, containing abodes of comparative bliss or of woe. In its neutral meaning, *hell* refers simply to the world of departed spirits, regardless of what their condition there is. It is a first cousin of the word *hole* and means "a cavity, the underworld, a hollow, subterranean place." In its positive meaning, it is used for the place of punishment. Thus, the wicked are spoken of as having gone to Sheol to endure torment and anguish (Psalms 9:16, 17; Deuteronomy 32:22).

In the word *Gehenna*—occurring twelve times in the New Testament, eleven of which are in the first three Gospels—we come across a picture word having a historic origin. It is a shortened term for the Vale of Hinnom, *Gê' Hinnōm,* a valley south of Jerusalem. The story of this place is told in 2 Chronicles 28:3.

In earlier days the Vale of Hinnom was a fair garden, but under two kings, became a place of idolatry. Little children were placed within a heated metal image, thus being made to pass through the fire, as an act of worship. Good King Josiah abolished this repulsive and cruel form of idolatry and defiled the Vale of Hinnom by making it the great rubbish heap of Jerusalem. Dead animals and unburied bodies of criminals were consumed therein. Fires continually burned, with an intense burning, on that immense pile. It was still used in this way in our Lord's day. In the third century A.D., it once more reverted to its original use as a garden. Today, the railway station of Jerusalem stands almost on the same site.

Christ clearly uses *Gehenna* as a name for the place of punishment for wicked men (Matthew 5:22, 29, 30; 10:28; 18:9; 23:15, 33). He did not mean the Gehenna burning outside the Jerusalem walls, but employed the term as a symbol of utter ruin. It means consignment to something equivalent to the great rubbish heap of Gehenna.

Then we have phrases like the "Lake of Fire," "the second death," "eternal punishment," "eternal fire," "eternal destruction," "outer darkness," "blackness of darkness" (Matthew 25:41–46; 22:13; 2 Thessalonians 1:9; Revelation 19:20; 20:1–15). Much discussion has been focused upon the words *eternal, everlasting,* and *forever.* Exponents of the Larger Hope Theory seek to show that these words are "age long," denoting a quality and not a duration. A full discussion of this can be found in *Human Destiny,* by Sir Robert Anderson. But biblical descriptions carry the air of finality. The New Testament expressions concerning the serious subject of future retribution refuse to be despoiled of their content by linguistic analysis or of their credibility by philosophical reasoning. They mean what they bear upon their faces and convey an intelligible and reliable—however awful—conception of the futurity of the impenitent. If heaven is unending, so is hell.

As Professor James Orr puts it:

> It adds to the terribleness of these sayings that, as before remarked, there is nothing to put against them; no hint or indication of the termination of the doom. Why did Jesus not safe-guard His words from misapprehension, if behind them there lay an assurance of restoration and mercy?

One may ask, with John Oxenham, in a reply to Andrew Jukes, whether, ". . . if Christ had intended to teach the doctrine of eternal punishment, He could possibly have taught it in plainer terms?"

The Necessity of Hell

Nicholas Caussin says:

> If there be a paradise for virtues, there must be a hell for crimes. No less does Hell contribute to publish God's omnipotency than Paradise. . . . The justice of the Sovereign will no less appear in the condemnation of the culpable than in the defence of the innocent.

Obedience, as seen in doing the will of God, means blessedness. Disobedience to that will entails chastisement. "Sin is both an insoluble riddle and a terrible fact in the freely created universe of the Holy God," says Bishop Moule. And sin, resolving itself in disobedience to the revealed will of God, has formed hell. All the theories seeking to mitigate the sufferings of the wicked forget the unfaltering decisiveness of the Christian doctrine of sin. As Professor Clow reminds us:

> All these theories are motivated by a terror of suffering, rather than by a horror of sin. We ignore the exceeding

sinfulness of sin. But not only with Jesus, but with the whole Scriptures it is sin, not suffering, which presents the torturing future to their minds. These theories are further shaken by the truth held in the cross, and the atonement of Christ. That truth is that sin against God is so deadly, and its consequences so awful, that it required the life and the passion of the Holy One to redeem man from his fate and grievous destiny.

Yes, and in a world where sin and truth are thoroughly seen, we want no other hell. Shallow views of sin and of God's holiness and of the glory of Jesus Christ and His claims upon us lie at the bottom of weak theories of the doom of the unpentitent.

When we see sin in all its hideousness and enormity, the holiness of God in all its perfection, the glory of Jesus Christ in all its infinity, nothing but a doctrine that those who persist in the choice of sin, who love darkness rather than light, and who persist in the rejection of the Son of God, shall endure everlasting anguish will satisfy the demands of our own moral intuitions. Men who eternally choose sin, should eternally suffer.

And with this solemn statement of Dr. R. A. Torrey I am in full agreement.

> It is full knowledge of the truth,
> When truth resisted long, is sworn our foe,
> And calls Eternity to do her right.
> AUTHOR UNKNOWN

The Arguments Against Hell

To be tenderhearted without being truthful is not loving. It is unkind. It is cowardly. Alas, however, the truth about hell is not told simply and clearly from the majority of the pulpits in our land. In fact, efforts are made to soften such a stern doctrine, for example:

There Is the Humanitarian Idea. The trend of modern thought is against the unalterable torment of the lost. A softer, humanitarian mind prevails. We are more concerned about the feelings of men than the facts of Scripture. And yet none was so kind as Jesus and none so stern in His language on hell. Although we have the broad record of the New Testament that, on the one hand, there is the unchanging felicity of those who have come into a loyal relationship with God and, on the other hand, the unchanging doom of the impenitent rebel, the bulk of preachers are silent about such truths, for fear of causing offense. And so, the thoughts of men are focused upon the life that now is. One trembles at the thoughts that the silence of some preachers is responsible for so much of the ignorance and indifference about the future and that these men are consequently not free from the blood of Christ-less souls in hell.

The Character of God. Many, remembering the justice and love of God, say with Alfred, Lord Tennyson:

> O, yet we trust that somehow good
> > Will be the final goal of ill,
> > To pangs of nature, sins of will,
> Defects of doubt, and taints of blood;
>
> That nothing walks with aimless feet;
> > That not one life shall be destroyed,
> > Or cast as rubbish to the void,
> When God hath made the pile complete.

But while these lines may contain beautiful sentiment, they are not the truth of Scripture. The common argument used against hell is that God is too kind, loving, gracious, and forgiving to allow men to be lost forever. Having infinite purity and infinite pity, inexhaustible love and enduring mercy, He will not let men perish utterly out of His hand. If He remained indifferent to the lost, if He allowed a soul to suffer in hopeless torment, if He were callous before an unalterable doom, He would not be the God and Father of our Lord Jesus Christ. But no arguments about the love and power of God to save to the uttermost can cancel the fact of the free will of man or the plain statements of the Bible—confirmed, beyond question, by the living Lord Himself—as to the awful fate of the finally impenitent. Just as men walk on streets, they equally mock at the voice of wisdom and the accents of love and treat the cross of Christ with scorn.

What reason is there to suppose that, if their impenitence persists in this world and God is in His heaven, their unbelief will not persist in the world to come? It is idle to say that the anguish of hell will make men repent. There are men in a living hell, here and now. Their vices are scourging cords, tormenting fires, avenging furies, torturing devils. Yet, though they suffer in spirit and soul and body, and though those whom they love suffer with them and through them, they do not repent. They love darkness, rather than light, for their deeds are evil.

Moreover, escape from hell does not depend upon the love and goodness of God, but upon the repentance of man. God does not consign men to hell. They go there on their own feet, by the use of free action, and only so. And it seems quite clear that the sinner who *stays* in hell does so in the same way as he goes, namely, by his own free choice. The walls of hell, then, are not of God's building. They are the fashioning of man's sin. It is therefore no disparagement to God's moral character that hell remains unchanged: "I would—ye would not."

The Final Defeat of God's Will. Because men cannot reconcile the sovereignty of God with the teaching of hell, they force the latter into the background or else explain it away. "We cannot reconcile God's love and the doctrine of hell," said one preacher, "therefore we drop out one of them—

hell." But surely justice and punishment are not irreconcilable!

Salvation Out of Hell?   Believing that men must suffer eternally for their sin does not impute unto God any display of temper or vindictiveness. A man who deliberately does evil on this side, idly trusting in the mercy of God, deserves all he gets on the other side. But will his crimes be generously overlooked? This is the question I want to answer.

In Luther's letter to Hansen von Rechenberg, he said: "God forbid that I should limit the time of acquiring faith to the present time. In the depths of the Divine mercy there may be opportunities to win it in the future state." This is a pious hope. But has it the guarantee of Scripture? No! Unquestionably it is established beyond all doubt that *every* man dying in sin is lost forever. The Lake of Fire is the eternal abode of the finally impenitent. Death produces no change whatever in a person's character. The man wakes on the other side, as he went to sleep on this side. Retribution continues there, as it commences here. The law of habit forges a man's hell.

Life is opportunity, and if man fails to use his opportunity down here, the door of life closes upon him. The Bible declares, with unfaltering voice, that death is the dividing line of opportunity. It urges right choice *now*. And what is hell, but this truth seen too late?

Because it is not God's will that they should perish, He gives to man not *a* chance, but *every* chance. The cross of Christ proclaims this beyond doubt, for in order that men *might* be saved, Jesus shed His precious blood, that men might not perish, but have eternal life.

False Ideas About Hell

There are theories and statements about hell, which shock our sense of justice, jar upon our intellects, hide the essential truth from us, as well as contradict the inner message of such a solemn theme. Here is a brief summary of these.

The Fate of the Heathen.   Many years ago, it was held that any man who had not heard of Christ's salvation and accepted Him as Saviour passed to eternal perdition. That conception aroused compassionate hearts to a fervid evangelism, both at home and abroad. Now, as there are still vast multitudes in heathen lands, who are out of Christ, what is to become of them? They are all to be accounted as lost! Surely not! For they cannot be judged by the revealed Word or measured by its standard, who have not even heard of its existence. At least this is the teaching of Paul in Romans 2:14, 15.

The Talmud has a saying to the effect, "When you hear of a death, say, 'Blessed is the righteous Judge.'" And as we think of the death of the dim millions of heathenism, we know that God, as the Judge of all the earth, will do right and that we shall all be tried by a more just Judge than man. As Bishop Moule states it: "It is well to remember that the judgment is not in our hands, but that God is both legislature and executive." In each one of the innumerable cases, the "Judge of all the earth will 'infallibly' do justly (Genesis 18:25). Nothing will be decided roughly and in the mass. No one will be condemned for ignorance of that which it was impossible for him to know."

Although the heathen is not doomed—seeing that he has obeyed the light he received—he has missed the highest; so it is imperative for us to take him the Gospel of God's dear Son, in order that he may share our full fruits of Christ's redemption.

The Injustice of Absolute Punishment.   It is affirmed by some that the absoluteness of punishment is unjust, in view of the facts of life. As Professor William Clow tells us:

Men recall the circumstances of many millions of human lives. They think of the strain and trial and disadvantage under which so many live from the cradle to the grave. They recall the inheritance of evil, the entail of a succession of progenitors who indulged ignoble passions, the legacies of a mind and a temper and of words, which made a vicious life almost a foregone conclusion. They think of the number of short, undisciplined, and frustrate years which are the portion of so many. They recall the environment of limitation and of seducing evil; the mean street, the narrow home, the squalor of the fireside, the drab days spent in the company of the vicious and obscene, the continual odds against truth and purity. To think of a fixed fate and destiny for these would, it is said, be not only unreasonable but vindictive.

And so we have the difficult question as to the fate of those who, through evil inheritances and hindering environments, have had no adequate opportunity of facing the claims of heaven upon their lives. How will God act towards such persons?

Well, it is necessary to bear in mind that a man's life has a moral value apart from any destiny and that, in the light of the Bible, his moral decisions have an eternal value. For by his moral decisions man enters into a relationship with God, which determines his destiny here and hereafter. And as the Gospel is God's message of redeeming love to guilty men, He will judge men according to their reception of it. As such an orthodox writer as Sir Robert Anderson puts it in *Human Destiny:*

> Half measures are impossible in view of the Cross of Christ. The day is past when God could plead with men about their *sins*. The controversy now is not about a broken law, but a rejected Christ. If judgment, therefore, be our portion, it must be measured by God's estimate of the murder of His Son.

But who are they who shall be held guilty of this direct sin? The answer is with God and not with us. If any who have heard the Gospel can prove that they are guiltless, we may be assured that the Righteous Judge will accept the plea.

The Question of Unbaptized Children. Perhaps there is no more brutal doctrine than that all unbaptized children go to perdition, simply because they are not baptized according to the rites of a particular church.

This is a monstrous, false doctrine, absolutely contrary to the character of God and opposed to the evangel of Christ. Augustine taught that all children dying unbaptized would certainly be damned. And in a book published a few years ago, the same heartless doctrine is expounded:

> Suppose a child die having committed a few sins through ignorance or temptation, of which it has not repented, the common doctrine is that the child will be burned in Hell fire to all eternity, and have devils, whoremongers, drunkards and liars for its companions.

Something of the same blasphemous and ghastly theology is found in a book by the Reverend Father Horace Howard Furniss. In his volume for children, entitled *The Light of Hell*, here is what he says:

> Little child, if you go to Hell there will be a devil at your side to strike you. He will go on striking you for every minute for ever and ever without stopping. The first stroke will make your body as bad as the body of Job. The second stroke will make your body twice as bad as the body of Job. The third stroke will make your body three times as bad as the body of Job. The fourth stroke will make your body four times as bad as the body of Job. How, then, will your body be after the devil has been striking it every moment for a hundred million years without stopping?

How different is the conception of Him who loved little children, saying of them: "Of such is the kingdom of heaven." Among the inhabitants of hell no children will be found. What a consoling thought this is! There are no dear babies in hell. Dying before they came to the age of moral responsibility and the power to discern between right and wrong, they pass right into the presence of Jesus, in virtue of His atoning work upon the cross. Original sin they do have, which is covered by the Blood. Practiced sin they have not and therefore are not guilty of transgressions incurring the wrath of God. The mentally disordered enter heaven— that is, if born insane—upon the same conditions as young children.

The Gradation of Punishment.   Another erroneous idea within the minds of some is that the lot of all who fail to accept the eternal life in Christ is all of one grade. But hell is not a place of uniform punishment, just as heaven is not a place of uniform reward and honor. The very terms *judge* and *justice* in themselves render uniformity of treatment for offenders impossible. Just as no state or people has administered the law on such lines, neither will Christ so administer justice, as passages such as Job 19:11; Matthew 16:27; 23:14; Romans 2:6; Revelation 20:13 so clearly prove.

Opportunity and its use and abuse are taken into account. Chastisement in hell is proportionate to the fault. There can be no one, common punishment, since the principle of equity declares that differences of guilt demand different degrees of chastisement. No judge would administer equality of punishment for inequality of crime, since that is unjust. And so, as Professor Orr tersely states it:

> The fullest weight must further be given to what the Scripture so expressly says of gradation of punishment, even of the unsaved. . . . There are "few stripes" and "many stripes" (Luke 12:47–48); for those then it will be

"more tolerable" than for others in the day of judgment
(Matthew 11:20-24). Even "Sodom and her daughters" will
be mercifully dealt with in comparison with others (Ezekiel
16:48-61). There will be for every one the most exact
weighing of privilege, knowledge, and opportunity. There
is a vast area here for the Divine administration on which
no light at all is afforded us.

Yes, and of this we are certain, that hell is not for the majority of the human race. On this point Dr. James Guthrie
well says: "My belief is that in the end there will be a vastly
larger number saved than we have any conception of."
What sort of earthly realm would that be where more than
half the subjects were in prison, suffering varying grades of
punishment? Hallelujah! Heaven is to contain "a great number no man can number."

> And would all be set to rights again
>   When God had gleaned a few,
> While the harvest of the nations
>   Was fagotted for fire?

Praise God! the harvest of the nations will not be fagots for
the fire of hell, but eternal followers of the Lamb.

The Fire of Hell.   We pass by many fanciful ideas of hell,
such as the Jews have in their Talmud, with its seven abodes
in hell, each abode having 7,000 caverns, each cavern 7,000
clefts, each cleft 7,000 serpents to bite the wicked, and other
representations to be found in the Koran and in various
heathen treatises.

Let us face the question regarding the fire of hell. Is it literal or symbolic?

John Milton is early responsible for the extreme teaching
of the eighteenth century, regarding the actual flames in
hell. Here are some of his passages from *Paradise Lost:*

Hither by harpy-footed Furies hail'd . . .
From beds of raging fire to starve in ice
Their soft ethereal warmth, and there to pine
Immovable, infix'd, and frozen round,
Periods of time; thence hurried back to fire.

Jonathan Edwards, who, when he preached about hell, could make the people grip their seats, lest they should tumble into its caverns, spoke of "a Lake of Fire in the centre of the world in which the wicked will lie sensible for ever and ever, with billows of fire always rolling over them." And, while we may think such language unjustifiable, we must not forget that God has been pleased to greatly bless and use such teaching, as to wit, the conversion of Mary Slessor, who became an extremely successful missionary to Africa.

The fire of hell, however, is not literal, but symbolic. Eternal fire cannot be harmonized with darkness, since fire implies a certain degree of light. Physically we cannot have total darkness and fire at the same time and in the same place. And, further, fire cannot kindle a spirit that is immaterial. The description *fire*, then, is figurative, signifying the pangs of guilt and remorse of conscience, which no expression can more fittingly describe than the undying worm and the unquenched fire. The conception of the literal fire and the literal worm may be rejected; but, what these mean for the body, something corresponding must be for the spirit. The experience must be worse than the figures expressing it. The fire is symbolic of retribution, the symbol of divine vengeance against evil. It stands also as a symbol of remorse and dissatisfaction. Even on earth, conscience and unrest can torture a man far more acutely than fire. Those two sides of the image represent two sides of the one truth: God is hostile to sin, and man suffers for committing it.

9

How to Prepare for Death and Destiny

In the previous meditations on dying and death, I endeavored to outline the significance and the opposite issues of death: namely, heaven and hell. A final word is necessary concerning the heart preparation we must cultivate for eternity, for any decision as to our eternal destiny is impossible beyond the grave.

To quote Professor Salmond, again:

> The recorded sayings of Christ bring two events, death and judgment, into relation, and give no disclosure of an intermediate state with untold potentialities of divine love and human surrender. They never traverse the principle that this life is the scene of opportunity, and this world the theatre of human fates. Such is the testimony which an unprejudiced exegesis has to offer.

Preparing the Way

The voice of Scripture describing this lifetime as being the only time in which our future after death can be chosen is unmistakably clear and emphatic: ". . . behold, *now* is the accepted time; behold, *now* is the day of salvation" (2 Corinthians 6:2, *italics mine*). Death completely ends such a day. Then there is the further warning, "How shall we escape [eternal condemnation and woe], if we neglect so great salvation . . . ?" (Hebrews 2:3). To these prophetic divine notices of a future state, we can add the solemn one of Jesus: "He that believeth on the Son hath everlasting life: and he that believeth not the Son shall not see life; but the wrath of God abideth on him" (John 3:36).

Two states, then, are declared as being absolute, fixed, and eternal: namely, the state of unbroken peace and unending joy in the presence of God, for the redeemed, or the sentence of banishment from God's presence and the beginning of a state of misery and dread.

While we are able—mentally and physically—how can we prepare to meet God, as the Prophet Amos entreats us to do? (Amos 4:12). Those who are heaven bound because they are heaven born, being saved from wrath to come, desire others to share in the eternal bliss of the redeemed. Thus, a personal and vital factor in their effort to lead those around to a realization of the necessity of heart preparation for eternity is the passion for souls begotten by the Holy Spirit, "Who will have all men to be saved, and to come unto the knowledge of the truth," (1 Timothy 2:4). Being saved to serve, these soul winners live under the impact of the petition:

> O God, to think the countless souls that pass away
>   Through each short moment that we live
> Destined to dwell in Heaven or groan in Hell for aye.
>   O stir me up, and new strength give,
> And let not one pass out through death in shame and sin,
>   That I through Thee might seek and win.
>
> AUTHOR UNKNOWN

Presenting the Gospel of Grace

Many years ago General William Booth, founder of the Salvation Army, addressed a company of his cadets and somewhat alarmed them, when he said, "I wish I could send you to Hell for two weeks, as part of your training." We know what he meant! To fully realize the doom of the impenitent and the lost would beget in those soldiers of his an undying desire to warn them "day and night with tears" to accept the Lord Jesus as their personal Saviour, seeing that He is the only avenue of escape from eternal death.

As those redeemed by blood, if we truly believe, as the Bible teaches, that men and women are to be eternally banished from the presence of God, if they linger and die in their sin, surely it behooves us to present to them the Gospel of the grace of God, prayerfully, earnestly, and believingly, agonizing lest they should miss so great salvation and eternally suffer the moans, sorrows, and regrets of the lost, in hell. Endeavoring to persuade sinners to change their manner of life, their master, and their destiny means attacking Satan's domain; and the keener we are to win souls from Satan for the Saviour, the more intense the antagonism and hatred of the enemy of God and man. And many faithful soul winners experience that the winning of souls is no easy task. As the hymn states it, their ". . . choicest wreaths are always wet with tears."

To be the means of snatching brands from the burning, the Christian must have an intimate knowledge of the plan of salvation, as well as a personal experience of God's power to emancipate the soul from the penalty and dominion of sin. There must also be the constant recognition of the fact that it is the Holy Spirit, and He alone, who can convict a sinner of sin, convince him of the efficacy of the Saviour's shed blood, and regenerate the soul. The secret of effective evangelism is to be found in the injunction, ". . . by my spirit, saith the Lord of hosts" (Zechariah 4:6).

First of all, the fact of sin must be stressed: ". . . all have sinned and come short of the glory of God" (Romans 3:23; *see also* Romans 5:12); "There is none righteous, no, not one" (Romans 3:10). All are sinners by birth, as well as by practice, and follow the Psalmist, who says, "Behold, I was shapen in iniquity and in sin did my mother conceive me" (Psalms 51:5). It must be firmly stated that good works or self-righteousness can never save a soul. If one is to be heaven bound, he must be heaven born. The one and only criterion determining a person's salvation and eternal destiny is his relationship to Jesus, who died as the Saviour of the world. Only the righteous in Him have hope in death (Proverbs 14:32).

Once the sinner is made conscious of his lost condition in the sight of a thrice-holy God, there must follow his confession of and repentance for his sin. The cry must come from his distressed soul, as it did from the publican of old, ". . . God be merciful to me, a sinner" (Luke 18:13). In commissioning His disciples, Christ instructed them to preach that men should repent, meaning that they should be genuinely sorry for their sin and forsake it (Mark 6:12). Jesus also taught that there is joy in heaven, when sinners repent (Luke 15:7). He also affirmed that He came to call sinners to repentance (Matthew 9:13; Mark 1:15). Repentance was also the apostolic call, "Repent ye therefore, and be converted, that your sins may be blotted out . . ." (Acts 3:19). Repenting sinners can be assured that, if they truly repent and confess their sins, God will cleanse them from all their iniquity (1 John 1:9).

Coupled with repentance, is faith. When Jesus set out to preach the Gospel of the Kingdom, He said, ". . . repent ye, and believe the gospel" (Mark 1:15). Referring to the preaching of John the Baptist, Jesus declared that many who heard him preach repented not, that they might believe (Matthew 21:32). When the jailer cried, ". . . what must I do to be saved?" Paul and Silas replied, ". . . Believe on the Lord Jesus Christ, and thou shalt be saved . . ." (Acts 16:30, 31). Repenting sinners are saved by grace, through faith (Ephesians 2:8). Thereafter Christ dwells in the heart of the redeemed sinner, by faith (Ephesians 3:17). With faith in the efficacy of the redemptive work of Christ for a world of sinners lost, comes the assurance that the repentant sinner is saved—not only from all past sins and from all conscious sin in the present, but from eternal separation from God, resulting from living and dying in sin. Believing in Jesus results in everlasting life, deliverance from all condemnation, and from eternal death (John 5:24).

When the earnest soul winner comes to deal with those who procrastinate and say, "Not now, but some other time," warning must be given of the folly and peril of delay. There may never be another time. Having no lease on life, the sinner may die suddenly and, dying in his sin, be lost forevermore. The solemn word of Scripture is "He that being often reproved hardeneth his neck, shall suddenly be destroyed, and that without remedy" (Proverbs 29:1).

Those of us who prayerfully seek to bring sinners to the Saviour must ever remember that it is not our persuasive words or presentation of the way of salvation that saves, but the Holy Spirit, who convicts of sin, regenerates, makes the Saviour real, imparts faith, and leads to surrender. Continued dependence upon the Spirit of truth is necessary, for it is He who is the unceasing heavenly Seeker of lost souls and the One who alone can save them. He is ever with the soul winner in the sacred task of warning sinners to flee from the wrath to come.

How untiring was the Apostle Paul in his endeavor to win souls for Christ! That he was fruitful in this preeminent task is evident from his ministry, as recorded in the Acts and in his epistles, when he speaks of his many converts as *children* (1 Thessalonians 2:7–11). In his quest for souls, Paul kept before him the Judgment Seat of Christ, with its reward—in the shape of a "crown of rejoicing"—for soul winning. To his spiritual children in Thessalonica, he could write, "For what is our hope, or joy, or crown of rejoicing? Are not even ye in the presence of our Lord Jesus Christ at his coming? For ye are our glory and joy" (1 Thessalonians 2:19, 20). How the apostle anticipated the thrill of knowing that all the souls won for Christ would share in the blessedness of heaven, because of his Spirit-inspired and faithful ministry! Unbounded joy was his as he contemplated that he would not stand before his Lord empty-handed, with no souls to his account, no stars in his crown. Paul's crown of rejoicing would be studded with jewels he had secured for the Master, who had completely revolutionized his entire life.

May God forgive us if we have been indifferent to our responsibility of winning souls for Him who has provided them with a perfect salvation! If we profess to be saved by grace, but are hugging to ourselves the knowledge and experience of Christ's saving power, failing to realize that we are saved to win others, what regret will be ours at the Judgment Seat of Christ, when rewards are dispensed to those who are faithful unto death! What a tragedy it will be to face the Lord with a saved soul, but a lost life! ". . . saved; yet so as by fire," as Paul expresses it (1 Corinthians 3:15). May grace and power be ours to earn ". . . a full reward" (2 John 8). This, then, is one of the practical aspects of our theme, dying and death. If we should go home to Glory by the way of the grave, God will give us grace to die in peace. What we presently need is grace to live victoriously—to be more than conquerors in our own hearts and lives and to share the risen power of Him, who ever seeks to make us fruitful branches of Himself, as the true Vine (John 15). If we live and labor in the light of eternity, then the Lord Himself, who died to save a lost world, will rejoice our hearts with the commendation: ". . . Well done, thou good and faithful servant . . . enter thou into the joy of thy Lord" (Matthew 25:21).

10
The Man Who Died for Me

Years ago I came across a painting that left a deep impression on my mind. The artist endeavored to portray Jesus as a young man, working at the carpenter's bench. Sitting for quite a while at His task, He felt the need of a brief relaxation and, standing up, threw out His arms to stretch Himself. As He did so, the sun, beaming in through the window facing Him, cast a shadow of a cross behind Him, over His tools and bench. The Gospels reveal that the moment He left His carpenter's shop for His brief, but dynamic, ministry of about three years, the shadow of the cross lay over His pathway. He lived and labored, ever conscious of the end for which He was born. The climax of Calvary was ever in thought and word.

Facing the Cross

A study of the utterances of Jesus also indicates that, as He neared the cross, His references to it became more numerous and revealing. An example of this can be found in the twelfth chapter of John—setting forth, as it does, foregleams of the Saviour's one increasing purpose. With your Bible open before you, trace with me the various aspects He declared concerning the cross He was to endure for our sakes.

The Cross and Its Glory. Speaking as if the cross was actually before Him, Jesus said, ". . . The hour is come, that the Son of man should be glorified" (John 12:23). *Glorified* seems a strange word to employ in reference to His brutal, shameful death on a tree. Yet it was repeatedly the term He used as He faced His decease at Jerusalem.

> "Father, glorify thy name." Then came there a voice from heaven, saying, "I have both glorified it, and will glorify it again."
>
> John 12:28
>
> These things said Esaias, when he saw his glory, and spake of him.
>
> John 12:41
>
> ... Jesus said, "Now is the Son of man glorified, and God is glorified in him."
>
> John 13:31, 32
>
> ... Jesus ... lifted up his eyes to heaven, and said, "Father, the hour is come; glorify thy Son, that thy Son also may glorify thee."
>
> John 17:1

Gory would seem a more fitting word to use than *glory*, as we gaze at the blood-bespattered body of Jesus, nailed to the cross. But the original word for *glorified* implies a *"revealing of hidden beauty,"* as when the sun breaks through a dark cloud and reveals all its glory to the earth. Both the Father and the Son were glorified at Calvary, for it was there "Mercy and truth met together; righteousness and peace kissed each other" (Psalms 85:10).

Divine justice and love were glorified by the cross bearing the crucified Son of God. It had been decreed "... the soul that sinneth, it shall die" (Ezekiel 18:4). Anyone found guilty of a crime by an earthly court of justice must pay the penalty imposed. God, however, in His wisdom, solved the problem as to how He could carry out the merited death for sin, yet forgive and save the sinner, who should have died. In His love, He provided His own beloved Son to bear away the sins of the whole world (John 3:16; 1 John 2:2).

Although Paul suffered persecution for the cross of Christ, he could yet glory in it. "But God forbid that I should glory, save in the cross of . . . Christ . . ." (Galatians 6:14). All redeemed by the precious blood of the Redeemer can join with the hymnist and sing:

> In the cross of Christ I glory,
> Towering o'er the wrecks of time;
> All the light of sacred story
> Gathers round its head sublime.
>
> JOHN BOWRING

The Cross and Its Fruit.   What a forceful illustration from nature it was that Jesus used to describe the principle that fruitage can only come from death: ". . . Except a corn of wheat fall into the ground and die, it abideth alone; but if it die, it bringeth forth much fruit" (John 12:24). In his great Resurrection chapter, Paul enlarges on the fact that death produces life more abundant: "Thou fool, that which thou sowest is not quickened, except it die" (1 Corinthians 15:36).

Corn, when buried in the earth, dies to its original form and life, but rises again a beautiful, bountiful sheaf of waving corn, beneficial to mankind. So Christ, as the corn of wheat, fell into the ground and died. Yet He rose again and for well-nigh two thousand years has reaped a most glorious harvest. Shortly after His ascension and the advent of the Holy Spirit on the day of Pentecost, about three thousand souls were saved on one day; and, thereafter, ". . . the Lord added to the church *daily* such as should be saved" (Acts 2:47, *italics mine*).

Throughout the Book of Acts, we witness the rising tide of salvation, with the church becoming a potent force in the world by the end of the first century. Today, there are countless multitudes of the redeemed in heaven and on earth—"a great multitude no man can number," who form the true church of the Living God. As we endeavor to win souls to Christ, we make Him to see the results of the travail of His soul and be satisfied.

Although the ceaseless ingathering of the lost is the fruit of His passion, we are so slow to learn that we can only bring forth much fruit as we die to sin and self. It is only as "we lay in dust, life's glory dead," as George Matheson expresses it, that "from the ground there blossoms red, life that shall endless be." As branches of the true Vine, we may be in dire need of the purging resulting in the bearing of more fruit (John 15:1–5). I recall seeing a motto on a sign board outside a dyer's establishment in England:

> *We dye to live,*
> *We live to dye.*

By changing a letter, we affirm the truth that spiritual death is basis of spiritual fruitage:

> *We die to live,*
> *We live to die.*

The Cross and Its Discipleship. Facing the great multitudes who followed Him, Jesus was most emphatic concerning the terms of true discipleship. If any follower rejected those terms, the ultimatum would be heard: "And whosoever doth not bear his cross, and come after me, *cannot be my disciple*" (Luke 14:27, *italics mine*). The same sacrificial discipleship is further emphasized by our Lord in the Calvary chapter before us, where we have a quartet of terms describing what He requires of His disciples: *Love, hate, serve, honor* (John 12:25, 26).

LOVE: *"He that loveth his life shall lose it. . . ."* The implication here is that, if life is lived without reference to God—

who is the Origin and Owner of life and therefore the One who should occupy and order it—then its full import is lost. To love the pleasures, honors, riches, and possessions of this life—or to get on in life, as many set out to do—is to choose the wrong objective, seeing that "man's *chief end* is to glorify God, and to enjoy Him forever." Many a Christian has a saved soul, but a lost life, simply because self became the center and circumference of his life.

> Live for self, we live in vain.
> Live for Christ, we live again.

As the Master personified the truth He taught, He constantly found life in losing it, not for its own sake, but as the channel of service in a world of need. Paul caught this vision of true discipleship, when, warned by the Holy Spirit of God of the imprisonments and afflictions awaiting him, he would meet them with the challenge:

> But none of these things move me, neither count I my life dear unto myself, so that I might finish my course with joy, and the ministry, which I have received of the Lord Jesus, to testify the gospel of the grace of God.
>
> Acts 20:24

HATE: *". . . he that hateth his life in this world shall keep it unto life eternal."*   What a contrast is here presented: loving and losing, hating and keeping! Too many hate their lives in a wrong way and end by suicide. But what actually is the kind of hatred of life resulting in life eternal? Solomon came to hate life because of his fruitless ambition (Ecclesiastes 2:18). Jesus made it clear that the term *hatred* is to be taken in a comparative sense, signifying a loving less than one's chief love. "Hate thine enemy. . . . Love your enemies . . ." (Matthew 5:43, 44). Commenting on what Jesus said about hatred of loved ones and of one's own life in Luke 14:26, *The Ryrie Study Bible* says, "This saying does not justify malice or ill-will towards one's family, but it means that devotion to family must take second place to one's devotion to Christ." If He has the preeminence in all things, then life will take its rightful position. Did not Paul elaborate on this aspect of hating life when he wrote of the love Christ manifested when He willingly sacrificed His life for our salvation? He says that "... they which live should not henceforth live unto themselves, but unto him which died for them, and rose again" (2 Corinthians 5:15). That the apostle practiced what he preached is evident in his declaration in his Philippian letter:

> But what things were gain to me, those I counted loss for Christ. Yea doubtless, and I count all things but loss for the excellency of the knowledge of Christ Jesus my Lord: for whom I have suffered the loss of all things, and do count them but *dung*, that I may win Christ.
>
> Philippians 3:7, 8, *italics mine*

SERVE: *"If any man serve me, let him follow me; and where I am, there shall also my servant be. ..."* We are saved to serve, but the service that results in constant fellowship with the Master issues from the two conditions we have just considered. Some there are who try to serve Christ, but who are not saved. There are others who profess to be saved, but who do not serve the Saviour. May we be found among the faithful number who "... serve the Lord Christ" (Colossians 3:24).

HONOR: *"... if any man serve me, him will my Father honour."* Can we confess that this God-honoring and God-honored discipleship is ours? As we survey the wondrous cross on which Christ died, do we count our richest gain but loss and pour contempt on all our pride? Does His supreme sacrifice demand our souls, our lives, our all? There is no other way by which we can merit the honor of God.

The Cross and Its Suffering. Our finite minds will never be able to fully grasp all that was involved, as the Holy One sacrificed Himself to bear the sins of the whole world. Yet although it is beyond human comprehension to unravel the mystery of the Gospel, we can believe and rejoice in the fact that, when Jesus died on the cross, it was not the greatest martyr of all time, but as your personal Saviour and mine.

> We may not know, we cannot tell,
> What pains he had to bear;
> But we believe it was for us
> He hung and suffered there.
>
> CECIL FRANCES ALEXANDER

It is in this frame of mind that we approach a further foregleam of Calvary—an utterance weighted with the sorrow and suffering of Him who bled and died for our redemption: "Now is my soul troubled; and what shall I say? Father, save me from this hour; but for this cause came I unto this hour" (John 12:27).

When Jesus said "Now" and "this hour," He spoke as if He had actually reached Calvary—the climax of His life and ministry. Let us examine the phrases that make up this sorrowful, yet challenging, verse:

"Now is my soul troubled. . . ." In previous days, the soul of Jesus was often troubled by the sins and prejudices of men and by their rejection of His love and claims. But He had reached the culmination of His heart anguish, for the sorrows of death were compassing Him about. He faced the fact that He must drain the bitter cup His Father had given Him, even to its dregs. Think of all that was involved as He drew near to His cross and then endured it!

In the travail of His soul was dark Gethsemane, and He came to it that we might not go to Gehenna, or hell. There were His physical sufferings and agonies—when His soul was exceeding sorrowful unto death—resulting in His perspiration of great drops of blood, staining His face and the ground. Jesus' fear of dying was the cup He besought His Father to save Him from. Calvary was the end for which He was born.

Perhaps the sorest personal sorrow Jesus experienced was that of His betrayal: not by an enemy—then He could have borne it—but by a disciple He had chosen, one who had been His companion and familiar friend, one with whom He had taken sweet counsel, and one He had accompanied to the house of God. For a paltry sum, Judas sold his Master to the priests who sought to kill Him, but his blood money brought the disciples' treasurer no satisfaction. It burned a hole—not only in his pocket, but in his heart. Judas tried to get rid of his ill-gotten pieces of silver, but failed and ended his tragic act by committing suicide.

As Jesus emerged from the anguish of Gethsemane, He faced a great multitude carrying swords and staves. They had been commissioned by the chief priests to capture a lonely, unarmed, and physically and emotionally exhausted man. The sign of a kiss, by which Judas identifed his Lord, was a further stab in Jesus' already troubled heart. Then came His arraignment before the high priest; the false accusations leveled against Him; the scourging; the spittle; the blows, giving Him a battered face; and amid such terrible indignities, the heartless denial of Peter, who had previously declared he was prepared to die for his Lord.

Added to all this shame and anguish there followed His mock coronation, with a crown of thorns, which, pressing into His head, gave Him a bloody countenance. Then, stripped of His clothes, there came the nailing of His hands and feet to the rugged cross, while it was laid out on the ground. As the tree was fixed into place, it wrenched the manacled limbs of the crucified one.

The hours of pain of body and mind, the exposure of a tortured frame to a watching crowd, the indescribable thirst, the cruel taunts of the mob who gloated over such a gory spectacle, and the feeling of being Godforsaken formed the intolerable burden Jesus bore on our behalf. Is it any wonder that God turned midday into midnight, covering the earth in darkness, thus shielding the sight of His bleeding, battered Son from a gaping crowd? How true are the lines of the poet E. C. Clephane:

None of the ransomed ever knew, how deep were the waters
    crossed;
How dark the night the Lord passed through, ere
He found the sheep that was lost.

The next phrase in the impressive verse before us is one we do not fully appreciate or interpret: "... what shall I say? Father, save me from this hour..." (John 12:27). True as it is that He was despised and rejected of men, the marvel is that because of the joy set before Him, He endured the cross and despised all its shame (Hebrews 12:2, 3). Can you not, therefore, catch the note of contempt and challenge in Christ's question: "... what shall I say? Father, save me from this hour...." This was as much as to say, "I know all about the horrible experiences awaiting Me, but do You think I want You to shield Me from them? I am not a coward, shrinking from such a brutal death. Do not expect Me to show the white feather of cowardice. I'll drink the last drop of the bitter cup." Pilate, convinced of Christ's innocence, sought desperately to prevent Him from dying as a criminal on a wooden gibbet, but Jesus courteously refused the governor's intervention. Other men were born to live, but He was born to die, and die He would, defiantly and triumphantly, as the world's Redeemer.

"... but for this cause came I unto this hour." This last

phrase was repeated, with an addition, when Pilate asked Jesus about the nature of His mission in the world. ". . . To this end was I born, and for this cause came I into the world . . ." (John 18:37). What an emphatic statement this is! But *this hour* He had in mind was the death of the cross, for He knew that He had come into the world as the Lamb slain before its foundation. In the dateless past, before the creation of man, God was able to look down the vista of yet-unborn ages and know that man, after his appearance, would sin and thus require a Saviour. As soon as man sinned, there came the promise and prophecy of his deliverance from the shackles of iniquity. "The seed of the woman shall bruise the serpent's head" (*see* Genesis 3:15).

As Jesus came as the seed of a woman—Mary's firstborn child—heaven proclaimed that He appeared as the Saviour, who was Christ and Lord. The cause for which He was born was a God-ordained one. It was His love that drew salvation's plan in a just eternity; it was not a scheme hurriedly conceived to meet an emergency. The cause He came into the world to pursue was not primarily to be an example or a social reformer, a renowned teacher or a martyr dying for truths ardently believed. The testimony of Scripture is most explicit: ". . . Christ Jesus came into the world to save sinners . . ." (1 Timothy 1:15). The end for which He was born was to provide for the spiritually dead; He gave *life*—and life in an abundant measure: ". . . the Son of man came . . . to give his life a ransom for many" (Matthew 20:28).

As you think of your present life and sphere, can you make the Lord's affirmation your own and confess, "To this end was I born, and for this cause came I unto this hour"? Is yours a God-planned life, lived in harmony with His will and purpose? How tragic it is to realize that so many are born into the world, live their entire lives in it, and then pass out into eternity without discovering God's design for their sojourn on earth! What a wretched existence! Jesus could come to the end of His days, declaring to His Father,

". . . I have finished the work which thou gavest me to do" (John 17:4). May our end be as His!

The Cross and Its Judgment. It is to be feared that too many of us are content with a partial conception of the nature and being of God. We are satisfied in thinking of Him as a God of love, of kindness, of pity, of mercy, as a gracious Father ever ready to welcome the prodigal and heartily forgive him. But God's justice, righteousness, and judicial authority are not such welcome phases of the divine character to dwell upon. Yet, throughout Scripture, He is presented as the God of judgment, as well as the God of peace and goodness. Says the Psalmist, ". . . verily he is a God that judgeth in the earth" (Psalms 58:11).

Among His judgments is the one Jesus refers to in seven words: "Now is the judgment of this world . . ." (John 12:31). The use of the adverb *now*, meaning "at this present time," emphasizes the cross as an actuality. Jesus spoke, not as if He was anticipating the cross, but as if it were already there and Himself upon it, enduring the judgment upon sin, which sinners themselves should have borne. Punishing sin, yet absolving the sinner, was a problem God alone in His wisdom could solve; and He did so by giving His Son to die as the sinner's substitute. His judicial death is the basis of justification for all who accept Christ as Saviour. A world of sinners lost and ruined by the Fall deserved the just condemnation of a holy God; and judgment came, not upon the world, but in the person of Christ. In man's place, condemned, He stood and sealed the pardon of sinners with His blood. "There is therefore now no condemnation to them which are in Christ Jesus . . ." (Romans 8:1).

Much more could be written of this substitutionary aspect of the cross, but, as the remarkable hymn by Mrs. A. R. Cousin, included in *The Keswick Hymn Book*, so vividly and perfectly deals with divine judgment upon sin, I herewith cite it in full:

O Christ, what burdens bowed Thy head!
  Our load was laid on Thee;
Thou stoodest in the sinner's stead.
  Didst bear all ill for me.
A Victim led, Thy blood was shed;
  Now there's no load for me.

Death and the curse were in our cup—
  O Christ, 'twas full for Thee!
But Thou has drained the last dark drop—
  'Tis empty now for me.
That bitter cup—love drank it up;
  Now blessings' draught for me.

Jehovah lifted up His rod—
  O Christ, it fell on Thee!
Thou wast sore stricken of Thy God.
  There's not one stroke for me.
Thy tears, Thy blood, beneath it flowed;
  Thy bruising healeth me.

The tempest's awful voice was heard—
  O Christ, it broke on Thee!
Thy open bosom was my ward,
  It braved the storm for me.
Thy form was scarred, Thy visage marred;
  Now cloudless peace for me.

Jehovah bade His sword awake—
  O Christ, it woke 'gainst Thee!
Thy blood the flaming blade must slake;
  Thy heart its sheath must be—
All for my sake, my peace to make,
  Now sleeps that sword for me.

For me, Lord Jesus, Thou hast died,
  And I have died in Thee;
Thou 'rt risen: my bands are all untied,
  And now Thou liv'st in me.
When purified, made white, and tried,
  Thy Glory then for me.

The Cross and Its Dominion.   Crucifixion, for an innocent man, was a most vicious and undeserved form of death; but for Jesus, in spite of its shame and pain and injustice, the death of the cross was a most victorious one. That was why, so near to its climax, He could throw down the gauntlet and declare: ". . . now shall the prince of this world be cast out" (John 12:31).

Modern historians have given us thrilling accounts of national wars through the last century or so, and from these military leaders continue to learn much. As a Britisher, I can remember the Boer War in South Africa, World War I, World War II; and, at this present warlike time, I am fascinated by Christ's prophecy that this end-time period before His return would experience ". . . wars and rumors of wars . . ." (Matthew 24:6). We seldom think of the Bible as a book of battles and wars, yet war drums never cease to beat throughout its sacred pages.

The phrase before is a divine declaration of the contest of all ages—a grim contest between the Prince of Peace and the Prince of Darkness, or between heaven and hell. It is a momentous conquest, affecting the history of the world and the lives of countless millions of souls through time and eternity. It was the battle of Calvary—with the death of the victorious warrior and His triumph over death and the devil— that gave birth to Christianity. Calvary was heaven's Magna Carta, for all time guaranteeing the sons and daughters of Adam's race the rights and privileges of the victory of the cross.

The prediction and promise of the outcome of the battle of all battles is given at the beginning of world history; early in man's story one of the contenders succeeded in winning the conquest over the other, resulting in the sorrow and disgrace of the world's first inhabitants. But, from this apparent defeat of heaven, came the first pronouncement of the subjugation of the adversary of both God and man: "The seed of the woman shall bruise the serpent's head" (*see* Genesis 3:15).

The moment of the challenge came when the Prince of Life entered the arena with the Prince of Demons and robbed him of his long-held power and authority; it is this act that the bruising of the head implies. It was then that Jesus entered the strong man's house, as He said He would and, binding him, robbed him of his goods (Matthew 12:29). It was at Golgotha that, through death, the bloodstained Victor destroyed the enemy that had the power of death—that is, the Devil (Hebrews 2:13, 14). "By dying, death He slew." This is proven by Christ's last word from the cross: *finished!* as the original expresses it. This was not the cry of a victim, as if He was relieved that His pain and anguish were at an end, but the triumphant shout of a Victor, which shook the caverns of darkness, causing all hell to tremble.

What was finished as Jesus died, surrendering His spirit to God? Was it not our emancipation from sin, bondage, and final penalty? The Resurrection of Christ was His receipt for our debt, paid at Calvary. From the time Satan was cast out of heaven for seeking to ape God—resulting in the birth of sin (Isaiah 14:12–17)—his princely rule, authority, and power were uncontested, until the Temptation; but the real battle was fought at Calvary, which was Satan's Waterloo. Since then he has been a defeated foe, and ours is the privilege and obligation of appropriating that victory, by faith. Now sin need not have dominion over us, for we can be more than conquerors, through the blood of the Lamb. Does not James remind us that, if we resist the devil, he will flee from us? (James 4:7).

Is ours the constant triumph that keeps the devil running? Another apt poem by Mrs. Cousin is a most impressive confirmation of the outcome of Calvary's conquest:

> To Thee, and to Thy Christ, O God,
>   We sing, we ever sing.
> For He the lonely wine-press trod
>   Our cup of joy to bring.

His glorious arm the strife maintained,
　　He match'd in might from far.
His robes were with the vintage stained
　　Red with the wine of war.

To Thee, and to Thy Christ, O God,
　　We sing, we ever sing.
For He invaded death's abode
　　And robbed him of his sting.
The house of dust enthralls no more,
　　For He is strong to save.
Himself doth guard that silent door,
　　Great Keeper of the grave.

To Thee, and to Thy Christ, O God,
　　We sing, we ever sing.
For He hath crush'd beneath His rod
　　The world's proud rebel king.
He plunged in His imperial strength
　　The gulfs of darkness down.
He brought His trophy up at length
　　The foil'd usurper's crown.

To Thee, and to Thy Christ, O God,
　　We sing, we ever sing.
For He redeem'd us with His blood
　　From every evil thing.
Thy saving strength His arm upbore,
　　The arm that set us free.
Glory, O God, for evermore
　　Be to Thy Christ and Thee.

The Cross and Its Magnetism.　There may be those who question where the attractive force is in gazing upon such a gory spectacle as the cross must have presented, with its grim burden of a man blood-bespattered, writhing in pain, and dying of thirst. It must have been a most repellent sight.

Yet we read of those who, sitting down, watched Him there. The sufferer Himself knew all about the agony and ignominy of the criminal's death that would be His, when He would be lifted up to die. And He said that the horrid event would be a *draw:* " 'And I, if I be lifted up from the earth, will draw all men unto me.' This he said, signifying what death he should die" (John 12:32, 33).

The first thing we note about this definite statement regarding the persuasive power of the wondrous cross is the way Jesus refers to Himself as the victim. He used the double pronoun, "... I, if I. ..." As repetition in Scripture represents emphasis, He desired to make clear exactly who was about to be crucified. Two thieves were to be His companions in death, but He was not a fellow who deserved such brutal punishment, as one of the thieves himself confessed: "... We receive the due reward of our deeds: but this man hath done nothing amiss" (Luke 23:41).

With us, the big *I* often means self-adulation, but it was never so with Jesus, the One who came as the divine *I AM.* Who was He then? (John 12:34). Why, He was the One who came as Emmanuel, as the Wonderful One in all things, as the Counselor, the Mighty God, the Everlasting Father, the Prince of Peace. At Calvary, He brought an end to the sway of the prince of this world. Jesus went on to say, "... the prince of this world cometh, and hath nothing in me" (John 14:30). Had Satan occupied any territory in Jesus, He would have been unable to secure the complete victory over him. With us it is different, for—saved though we may be—we retain the old sinful nature we inherited, which is ever the advantage ground of Satan. But Jesus was born of Mary as "that holy thing."

Then He went on to describe the form of His death. He was to be *lifted up.* In His conversation with Nicodemus, Jesus used the illustration of Moses displaying a serpent on a pole, to enforce the manner of His imperative, beneficial death: "As Moses lifted up the serpent in the wilderness, even so must the Son of man be lifted up: That whosoever believeth in him should not perish, but have eternal life" (John 3:14, 15). In the checkered history of Israel, we have the incident in which the people grumbled against God and Moses for the mean fare the wilderness provided. Judgment came upon their murmuring, in the form of serpents that caused much death and destruction in the camp. But the lost repented of their sin; and deliverance was divinely provided, in the form of a serpent of brass, raised upon a pole. All bitten by serpents and thereby facing death looked up at God's remedy, and they lived.

Jesus saw in this dramatic episode a forceful type of deliverance for all bitten by that "Old Serpent, the Devil." Like the brazen serpent—made in the likeness of the death-dealing serpents—Jesus—made in the likeness of men, sin excluded—was also made sin for them. He employed the word *must*, for there was no other way by which sinners could be delivered from death. Since the cross, all who have looked at Him—or believed—have passed from death unto life. So sing:

> There is life for a look at the Crucified One,
> There's life at this moment for thee.
>
> AMELIA M. HULL

To the antagonistic Pharisees, Jesus said, ". . . When ye have lifted up the Son of man, then shall ye know that I am he . . ." (John 8:28). Here He is charging the Pharisees for being humanly responsible for His death. Theirs were the wicked hands that slew and crucified Him who is both Lord and Christ (Acts 2:23).

The Son of Man was *lifted up*, but not upon a golden pedestal, to be admired and applauded by adoring multitudes, worshiping Him because of His beauty and bounty. No, His throne was a rough and rugged cross; His crown one of thorns, with their blood-producing property; His royal attendants, two thieves dying for their crimes; His subjects, a yelling mob, taunting Him to prove He was God by delivering Himself from dying, even as He had saved others from death. Yet think of it! Such an exaltation as being slain and hanged upon a tree is the greatest draw the world has ever known.

Christ emphasized the claim of what He would accomplish by His cross: "I . . . will draw all men unto me. . . ." All humanity, irrespective of sex, age, race, color, condition, or position, would come to experience the compelling power of His cross, seeing He was dying to save the world (John 12:47). Countless multitudes of the redeemed in heaven and on earth join with C. M. Irons in the singing of his hymn:

> Drawn to the Cross which Thou hast blest
> With healing gifts for souls distrest.
> To find in Thee, my life, my Rest,
> Christ crucified, I come.

As a youth of eighteen, some seventy-six years ago, in 1904, I attended an evangelistic meeting. "I saw One hanging on a tree" for my salvation and, opening the avenues of my being to Him who hung and suffered there, my whole life was transformed, for:

> He drew me, and I followed on,
> Charmed to confess the Voice divine.
>   PHILLIP DODDRIDGE

Through the many years of my pilgrimage, my heart has been fired with gratitude, as I have constantly sung with John Bunyan:

> Blest cross! blest sepulchre! blest rather be
> The Man that was there put to shame for me.

What about you, my dear reader? Has Jesus drawn you to Himself? Have you given back the life you owe Him, because of the death He died for you? It matters not who or what you are or whether your name is inscribed on any church roll. The all-important question is: Will your name be found written in the Lamb's Book of Life? Is the Lamb who bled and died at Calvary your personal Saviour? If not, then what more effective prayer could come from your sin-stricken heart than that enshrined in the following appealing lines?

> Just as I am, without one plea,
> But that Thy blood was shed for me,
> And that Thou bidd'st me come to Thee,
> O Lamb of God, I come! I come!

11
Things Missing in Heaven

Having already considered heaven's reality and revelation as one of the two abodes awaiting those who leave the earth, we are now to examine several of this present world's characteristics that are missing from the "land of pure delight, where saints immortal reign."

No More!

John assures us, in his description of heaven, that within it all former things are passed away. While the apostle, by the Holy Spirit, unfolds something of the glory and magnificence of the Father's home, he appears to lean toward negatives, rather than positives. He tells us what is *not* there, rather than what *is* there. These things, which our lives are so wrapped up in here below, are given by John as a series of "no mores," which I shall now trace in the order he states them.

No More Hunger or Thirst (Revelation 7:16). Our glorified bodies will not require the natural means of subsistence we are now accustomed to. The Lord is to be our entire source of life (Revelation 7:16; 21:6). The difference between being hungry and suffering from hunger must be noted. As I pen these lines, it is near lunchtime, and I am feeling hungry; in a few minutes I will turn from writing to eating. Praise God, because there will be sufficient to eat. But suppose there was nothing to eat—not only today, but in days to follow. My hungry feeling would turn to hunger: the most dreaded experience of those who live in famine-stricken areas of the world and of the heartbroken refugees forced to flee from their home country. The glorious prospect of the redeemed, however, is stated by John: "They shall hunger no more. . . ."

The same blessed aspect of absence applies to sufficient water, so necessary to our existence on earth; not only will there be no hunger, but ". . . neither [will they] thirst any more. . . ." The children of Israel pleaded with Moses to provide them with water, for many were dying of thirst in the wilderness. But the old-time prophecy reads, "They shall not hunger nor thirst . . ." (Isaiah 49:10); in heaven we will be fulfilled in Him who is to be our eternal meat and drink. "For the Lamb which is in the midst of the throne shall feed them, and shall lead them unto living fountains of waters . . ."; ". . . I will give unto him that is athirst of the fountain of the water of life freely" (Revelation 7:17; 21:6). Christ will be our unfailing Bread of Life and the Smitten Rock, from which the perennial life-giving water will flow.

No More Sea (Revelation 21:1).   Lovers of the sea and sea dwellers may give vent to a sigh of regret as they read, ". . . and there was no more sea." But as the Creator of the new heaven and the new earth, who is replacing the present heavens and earth, God knows what is best for His new creation. Dante Gabriel Rossetti, poet of the nineteenth century, in his verse "The White Ship" has the phrase, "The sea hath no king but God alone." The Psalmist would have us know that "the sea is his, and he made it . . ." (Psalms 95:5). As the Sovereign Lord, He has the prerogative and power, not only to fashion the sea, but also to abolish it and create His eternal universe to exist without it. Jesus could walk on the sea and was able to change its turbulence into a great calm, with the command, "Peace, be still!"

The end of two features will make the absence of the sea desirable: namely, sorrow and separation.

THERE IS SORROW.   What tragedy and anguish are associated with the sea! The sixteenth-century poet Richard Barnfield wrote of one, "The waters were his winding sheet, and the sea made his tomb." Then we have William Whiting's great hymn, "Eternal Father, Strong to Save," in which there is the couplet:

> O hear us when we cry to Thee,
> For those in peril on the sea.

I still have a vivid recollection of one of the most tragic sea disasters in British history. It was in April 1912 that the Mistress of the Seas, as the nation was then known, launched the mightiest and most magnificent ocean liner ever built: the *Titanic.* As she glided slowly out of Southampton docks, on her maiden voyage, the large, admiring, and excited crowd that had gathered to bid the masterpiece of shipbuilding *bon voyage*, cried, "There she goes, and God Almighty cannot sink her." But, when out on the wide sea, headed for New York, the supposedly unsinkable ship plowed into a mountainous iceberg, was almost immediately crushed, and sank. Hundreds of passengers, who were dancing and drinking at the time, had no warning of a disaster and perished in a watery grave. Thus, the pronouncement, ". . . no more sea" can suggest the removal of its peril and tragedy forever. The time is coming when the sea will give up its dead (Revelation 20:13).

THERE IS SEPARATION.   Somehow I feel that this was the feature associated with the sea that John had in mind when he wrote of its abolition. There he was, in his cave, a prisoner on the Isle of Patmos, with the sea surrounding it. Cut off from the churches he had founded and nurtured in the faith, cut off from the many saints who loved him, John longed, in his forced isolation, to be reunited with those he loved and knew so well. He lifted up his eyes and beheld a vision of the New Jerusalem, and we can almost hear his sigh of relief as he penned the phrase, ". . . there was no more sea," implying the end to the absence of the Lord's people one from another. Nobody and nothing will be able to separate the redeemed from the Lord or from one another. They will then be together forever!

No Temple Therein (Revelation 21:22). The world has had—and still has—its magnificent temples, cathedrals, and ornate churches. But, while some of the innumerable churches have preserved the unity of the faith, there is not uniformity, since churches revolve around denominational differences and are not, ideally, one in Christ Jesus. So we have the Baptist Church, the Presbyterian Church, the Methodist Church, the Anglican Church, the Lutheran Church, and so on.

But in heaven I will not be in my little corner, eating my Baptist pie; nor will you be in your small corner, eating your Presbyterian or Lutheran pie. There are no religious distinctions or sects in the Glory land. All who are there, irrespective of their religious labels on earth, are only known there as sinners saved by God's matchless grace. The great multitude that no man can number—a multitude out of all nations and kindreds and people—will stand before the throne and before the Lamb, and they shall be clothed in robes made white by the blood of the Lamb (Revelation 7:1–17).

Heaven itself will be the vast, glorious temple in which the angelic and redeemed hosts will eternally worship and serve the Triune God in sincerity and truth. These ". . . serve him day and night in his temple . . ." (Revelation

7:15). John, as we shall find, tells us there is "... no night there ..." (Revelation 22:5). But there is no contradiction here, for "day and night" is figurative language in Scripture, implying ceaseless, unending service. The further truth is that "... the Lord God Almighty and the Lamb are the temple [in heaven] ..." (Revelation 21:22). Not only so, "... the tabernacle of God is with men, and he will dwell with them, and they shall be his people ..." (Revelation 21:3).

No Sun, No Moon, No Candle, No Night (Revelation 21:23; 22:5; 18:23; 7:16). How absolutely dependent we are upon two modes of illumination: natural and artificial light. Only one-half of the world has light at a given time. But, in heaven, the Lord, who created the sun to rule by day and the moon by night, will be the eternal illumination. He will diffuse light everywhere at the same time. Such eternal light is outside the scope of scientific investigation. It transcends our human, finite comprehension. What a brilliant, eternal city heaven is, even though it has no lamps, no sunrises, no sunsets! It has no sun, moon, or stars providing natural light; and no candle, oil lamp, gas, or electricity gives artificial light, when darkness reigns. Darkness is simply the absence of light. In heaven, "eternal light excludes the night."

When Jesus was on earth, He could confess, "... I am the light of the world ..." and He functions as the Light in the world above. In heaven, there is no sun to scorch with burning heat (Revelation 7:16), no shining candles or lamps (Revelation 18:23). The glory of God lightens the city, and the Lamb is the Light (Revelation 21:23). Since there is "no night there," with its darkness, fear, terror, and crime—for men love darkness, rather than light, because of their evil deeds—the assurance is that the Lord God giveth them light.

No More Sin (Revelation 21:27). Presently, we live in a sinful world that is waxing worse and worse—a world controlled by its satanic god. But our glorious hope is that of living in a sinless world, in which there will be no devil to tempt and destroy its inhabitants. "And there shall in no wise enter into it any thing that defileth, neither whatsoever worketh abomination, or maketh a lie . . ." (Revelation 21:27). It is not only a world without sin, but also a world without unsaved sinners. Its only citizens are those whose names are written in the Lamb's Book of Life. Outside the city are ". . . dogs, and sorcerers, and whoremongers, and murderers, and idolaters, and whosoever loveth and maketh a lie" (Revelation 22:15).

Whether we are among those saved by grace and are in the city of pure delight, or whether we are outside its pearly gates, in eternal darkness, because of our unsaved condition and a heart destitute of the presence of the Lamb, depends upon our decision while in this sinful and sinning world. What we are when we die, we remain throughout eternity. It is the fixity of character that John reminds us of when he says, "He that is unjust, let him be unjust still: and he which is filthy, let him be filthy still: and he that is righteous, let him be righteous still: and he that is holy, let him be holy still" (Revelation 22:11). It is because heaven is the holy Jerusalem that there are missing the following features which are more or less related to sin.

No More Death (Revelation 21:4). Being a sinless habitation, heaven knows no death. There life is eternal. The Lamb is all the glory in Immanuel's land; for, having destroyed the devil, who had the power of death, He has provided a deathless world for His redeemed ones. Think of it: no dying, no death, no separations because of death, no graveyards!

No Sorrow (Revelation 21:4). Shakespeare, in *Richard II*, has the poignant phrase, "Write sorrow on the bosom of the earth"; and what a sorrowful world it is—one to which Jesus came and, in it, was the Man of Sorrows, acquainted with human grief. We have self-produced sorrows and sorrows caused by others. There are other sorrows, divinely permitted, as Eve—who suffered the first sorrowing heart on earth—proved. Hers was a sorrow that came because of sin (Genesis 3:16). Since then many have ". . . pierced themselves through with many sorrows," and continue ". . . to eat the bread of sorrows . . ." (1 Timothy 6:10; Psalms 127:2). But in heaven there are no sorrowing hearts. In a true sense, they ". . . see no sorrow" (Revelation 18:7), for their sorrow is turned into joy (John 16:20).

No Crying (Revelation 21:4).   Because we live in a tear-drenched world, what a happy prospect awaits us; for no eyes are wet with weeping in the summer land up yonder. Now, "My tears have been my meat day and night . . ." and God assures me that He does not forget my tears, but stores them up in His bottle (Psalms 42:3; 56:8). There are those who appear to be too hard and dry to cry. Yet we should never be ashamed or afraid to weep, for often our tears are as a telescope, bringing us a clearer vision of the "morn that tearless be." Paul served the Lord continually, with many tears (Acts 20:19). The woman of Nain, who was a sinner, washed the feet of Jesus with her repentant tears (Luke 7:44). We are exhorted to weep with those who weep (Romans 12:15).

Missing, in heaven, are the tears of Jesus. Alive forevermore, as the glorified Son of God, He weeps no more. But, on the earth, His eyes were often wet with tears. Did He not mingle His warm tears with those of the sorrowing relatives and friends of Lazarus? One of the most pathetic phrases in the Gospels is, "Jesus wept" (John 11:35). Those who saw Him cry said that His tears were those of love. He could weep over the sin, as well as the sorrow, of others. Facing His rejection by those of Jerusalem, the so-called holy city, we read that ". . . he beheld the city and wept . . ." (Luke 19:41). The Gospels reveal Jesus as a man of prayer; and His prayers, says the writer to the Hebrews, were offered up with ". . . strong crying and tears . . ." (Hebrews 5:7).

The next time your cheeks are tearstained, remember, as you experience their dripping rain, that Jesus died and rose again, that His own might never weep again, once they crossed the world's river of tears. He shed both tears and blood, so that His redeemed ones might have dry eyes forever. God also is to take His fragrant handkerchief and wipe away all our tears (Isaiah 25:8; Revelation 7:17; 21:4).

No Pain (Revelation 21:4). The patriarch of old wrote about those who travail with pain all their days (Job 15:20). Wordsworth also reminds us about many who are ". . . doomed to go in company with Pain. . . ." Ours is a world in which it is almost impossible to find a life that has not suffered pain of some sort. Universal and persistent pain led to the provision of drugs, pills, and opiates, as measures of relief. Pain is no respecter of any part of our persons. Its ache can strike us as it did the prophet, when he wrote, ". . . I am pained at my very heart . . ." (Jeremiah 4:19). It can disturb the mind. John Keats reminds us of "the troubled sea of the mind," and mental torment is a dreaded aspect of pain. More common is physical pain, which is the herald, the warning, and the location of some bodily disorder.

The eternal pain Matthew Arnold described is only related to those who die in their sin. Jesus spoke of the rich man in hell, "being in torments." So many of the Lord's people are bedridden, with pain as their constant companion. Others, who may be mobile, take pain in their strides. But for all suffering saints, there is the promise and prospect of a glorified body that pain can never afflict. One moment of heavenly bliss will obliterate unnumbered hours of earthly pain.

> There is a land of pure delight
> Where saints immortal reign
> Eternal Light excludes the night
> And pleasures banish pain.
>
> IRA SANKEY

No Curse (Revelation 22:3; Genesis 3). It is generally known that the Bible begins and ends with gardens. What is not realized as it should be, is that the curse associated with the initial garden is missing from the last garden. John describes the final garden as having a crystal river and health-yielding fruits, all of which are for, not the *healing* of the nations—seeing there are no sicknesses requiring healing properties—but for the *health* of the nations. In the Garden of Eden there was one tree that God forbade Adam and Eve to pluck fruit from or even touch; but Eve knew its fruit was nutritious, as well as beneficial to the mind. Such a participation brought a curse upon Satan, as well as a curse upon the human race and the expulsion of our first parents from the garden (Genesis 3). ". . . Cursed is every one that continueth not in all things which are written in the book of the law to do them" (Galatians 3:10).

The glory of the Gospel, however, is the blessed fact that Christ took our curse and made it His own. "Christ hath redeemed us from the curse of the law, being made a curse for us: for it is written, Cursed is every one that hangeth on a tree" (Galatians 3:13; *see also* Deuteronomy 21:23). Curse and death came through a tree, but, at Calvary, blessing and life came through Him who hung on a tree. The cross turned the curse into a blessing—an evidence of God's love (Deuteronomy 23:5). How thrilled John was when—with earth's first garden and its curse in mind—the Lord gave him a glimpse of the heavenly garden, in which there was no more curse. Added joy was his when he was assured that he would again see the face of Him who bore his curse (Revelation 22:1–4).

From other Scriptures, one can discover other things that are barred from heaven. For instance, Job would have us know that "There the wicked cease from troubling; and there the weary be at rest" (Job 3:17). The reason why the wicked cannot trouble the saints at rest in heaven is because they are eternally excluded from such a blissful abode. ". . .

do ye not know . . . the wicked is reserved to the day of destruction? they shall be brought forth to the day of wrath" (Job 21:29, 30; *see also* Revelation 21:8; 22:15).

Also absent from heaven are the marital relationships God ordained at the beginning (Genesis 2:24; Matthew 22:30). Our glorified bodies will not have the physical differences characteristic of male and female, as here on earth.

12
Some May Never Die

Many who read this chapter title may question its reality, since we read that "death hath passed upon all men" and we know that the majority of people prepare, in some way or another, for their departure from this mortal scene. Yet the fact remains that millions now living may never die. The Advent hymn has the line:

> O joy! O delight!
> Should we go without dying

And we may! When Jesus comes for His church, all who are His will not taste death, but be caught up to meet the Lord, in the air. What a blessed hope this is!

The Second Advent

Paul's epistles are saturated with the truth of the Second Coming of Christ. More than any other New Testament writer, he can be called the Apostle of the Advent. Directly taught by the Holy Spirit, it is Paul who brings us a full revelation of the various aspects of our Lord's appearing. His two letters to the Thessalonians are particularly devoted to the church's Rapture and earth's conditions thereafter. Taken together, these remarkable epistles cover the two stages of Christ's return. The first epistle deals with our

Lord's coming for His church. In the second epistle, Paul describes characteristic features of the Tribulation.

Perhaps you have noticed that, at the end of each chapter in the first epistle to the Thessalonians, Paul concludes with some aspect of the Second Advent. He employs the "blessed hope," to give emphasis to his manifold exhortations, counsel, and warnings. Broadly, we can outline the five chapters thus:

Chapter 1:9, 10 associates our salvation and patience with the return of Christ: "For they themselves shew of us what manner of entering in we had unto you, and how ye turned to God from idols to serve the living and true God; And to wait for his Son from heaven, whom he raised from the dead, even Jesus, which delivered us from the wrath to come." (*See also* Psalms 49:15.)

Chapter 2:19, 20 connects service and its reward with the coming of Jesus: "For what is our hope, or joy, or crown of rejoicing? Are not even ye in the presence of our Lord Jesus Christ at his coming? For ye are our glory and joy."

Chapter 3:12, 13 has conduct in view: Love—Godward and manward—is prominent in this chapter: "And the Lord make you to increase and abound in love one toward another, and toward all men, even as we do toward you: To the end he may stablish your hearts unblameable in holiness before God, even our Father, at the coming of our Lord Jesus Christ with all his saints."

Chapter 4:13, 18 declares the Second Advent to be the spring of all our comfort: "But I would not have you to be ignorant, brethren, concerning them which are asleep, that ye sorrow not, even as others which have no hope.... Wherefore comfort one another with these words."

Chapter 5:23 outlines the character of the saint and reveals the sanctifying influence of the Advent: "And the very God of peace sanctify you wholly; and I pray God your whole spirit and soul and body be preserved blameless unto the coming of our Lord Jesus Christ."

Looking more closely at these five chapters, we discover that Paul reminded the Thessalonians of a five-point relationship they had to preserve and practice, in view of Christ's return.

As a Believer (1:9, 10). Here the believer is viewed as a waiting one, and patience appears to be the quality he must exhibit, seeing Christ is at hand. There are three words used by Paul to indicate a full-orbed life! They are *turn, serve, wait.* Some turn, but they do not serve. Others serve, but never learn to wait. Salvation, occupation, and expectation, however, go together. Going back to 1:3, we have an illuminating commentary on Paul's description of those Thessalonians he was the means of winning for the Lord. He gives us a triad:

Their work of faith, turning to God from idols—past
Their labor of love, serving the living and true God—
    present
Their patience of hope, waiting for His Son from
    heaven—future

Thus faith rests on the past; love works in the present; hope endures as seeing the future. The inclusion of *serving* proves that the Advent does not cut the nerve of effort, but strengthens one for all legitimate labor.

One reason why the church is flirting with the world is because she has put out of her mind (if ever she had it in there) the expectation of God's Son from heaven. She has activity in plenty, but the third part of her attitude is missing. It is said that Michelangelo, by his prolonged and unremitting toil upon frescoed domes, acquired such a habitual upturn of countenance that, as he walked the streets, strangers, observing his bearing, set him down as being somewhat visionary and eccentric. If, as professing Christians, our conversation is truly in heaven, our faces will be set hitherward. Instead of having our eyes fastened on the ground—like the man with the muck rake, whom John Bunyan describes—we will walk the dusty paths of life with an upward look. Our eyes will be upon the coming dawn.

As a Worker (2:19, 20). Here the believer is presented as the serving one, and joy resulting from faithful ministry is prominent. One translation has it, "It is the thought of presenting you to Him that thrills me with joy, hope and pride, the thought of wearing such a decoration before Him." Paul is here declaring that, at the Judgment Seat of Christ, he will be prouder of his converts than a king of his crown and a champion of his laurels. The apostle expresses a similar joy in 2 Corinthians 1:14 and Philippians 4:1.

There are crowns to earn, but this "crown of rejoicing" is the one acting as an incentive to service. What a thrill will be ours to realize that souls will be at the bema because of our influence and testimony here below. Would it not make for a mighty revival, if every believer truly lived and labored in the light of Christ's return? Are we as jealous as we should be over the winning of our own loved ones for the Lord? Mother, what about your daughter? Father, what about your boy? Christian worker, Sunday-school teacher, what about those around you? Will others greet your Saviour, because of your faithful witness?

Possibly you have all the heart could wish for, here on earth: a comfortable home, a well-appointed sphere, the absence of poverty or loneliness. But what of the future? Will you experience the joy and thrill of the apostle? Will there be any stars in your crown, when at evening the sun goeth down? Or will yours be a joyless meeting with the Saviour, the reception of a starless crown—an entrance, empty-handed, into His presence? As we have not long to live, let us solemnly ask ourselves what joy and triumph will be ours when we see Jesus. God forbids that any of us should get just inside Glory: saved by faith, but nothing to our credit, no service to reward! May we hasten the Crowning Day by gathering in the lost ones for whom the Saviour died!

As a Brother (3:12, 13).   Here the believer is brought before us as a loving one, and *love*—Godward and manward—is emphasized. "The Lord multiply you in love until you have enough and to spare of it." Well, there is not too much to spare of love among Christians today! Paul's exhortation can be translated, "So that you may not only love one another abundantly, but all mankind." Can we say that we are the true brothers and friends of all Christ's little ones? What shame will be ours as we meet the gaze of Christ, if we have not been kind to the household of faith! Paul points to his own example as he urges others to love. Night and day, he thought of others. As a nurse Paul had cherished the needy (2:7). And he here emphasizes brotherly love as the evidence of a life of holiness. A loveless heart can never succeed in the quest after holiness, for true love sanctifies the one who loves.

As the shadows gather, Paul would have us increase and abound in love or, as Dr. Weymouth puts it, "growing and glowing in love." Alas, the growth and glow of love is not being generally experienced by the Lord's people! Love's fruit is frosted. Paul prays that the Thessalonians might love one another in a superlative degree. He desires them to overflow with love. As we get nearer the return, it would seem as if the devil is active, drying up the spring of love, for never was there such an unloving attitude manifested among professing Christians. We sing about knowing each other better, when the mists have rolled away, but why wait until the future for a full recognition? We must endeavor to know each other better here and now. In this epistle Paul tells us that we must be at peace among ourselves (5:13). He urges the Thessalonians to greet one another with a holy kiss, which was a way of expressing love. Now we feel more

like *kicking* some Christians than kissing them! And yet a revival of love among God's people, in view of Christ's coming, would make for a mighty ingathering of lost souls. "By
this shall all men know that ye are my disciples, if ye have
love one to another" (John 13:35).

As a Sufferer (4:13-18). Here the believer is portrayed as
the weeping one; and comfort, in view of the separations of
life, is stressed by the writer.

The Thessalonians were troubled over those who had
died. Recently converted from their heathenism, they were
still haunted by the pagan ideas of the future. A heathen in-
scription discovered in Thessalonica reads:

> After death no reviving—
> After the grave no meeting again.

And so Paul sends this letter, assuring troubled hearts
about the heavenly felicity and future resurrection of their
holy dead. All who died in Christ are presently with Christ
and will return with Him, to assume glorified bodies. Thus
all the sorrows, sufferings, and separations are lifted up and
placed alongside "the blessed hope" and thereby robbed of
their sting.

Because the unseen world is perpetually opening to receive those we love, we continually need the comfort of
Paul's Advent truth. Amid the partings and farewells of life,
so common in times of brutal war, we do not sorrow, as
others, who have no hope. Weeping over those who have
left us, we do not weep for them. A blissful reunion awaits
the Lord's people:

> . . . Some from earth, from glory some,
> Severed only 'Till He come!
>
> EDWARD H. BICKERSTETH

Alas, secular life today is almost as hopeless as the paganism Paul corrected. The multitudes around have their attention fixed on the present world and studiously avoid all distraction of the future. Determined to have a good time now, they are willing to risk their chances in the world to come. The saints of God, however, do not grasp things of earth, seeing they may leave them at any moment, to meet Jesus in the air. And as this old world ripens for judgment, let us comfort one another with the words of the coming shout and trump and voice.

As a Saint (5:23).   Here the believer is brought before us as a holy one, and complete sanctification is the application Paul makes as he again stresses the coming of Christ. And what a fitting climax this is for his Advent epistle! Paul calls the believer to be saintly in life. He must be separated from sin and dedicated to the service of the Lord. The question of paramount importance is: When Jesus comes, will He be pleased with the holiness of my life, the simplicity of my obedience, and the faithfulness of my service?

"May the God of peace consecrate you through and through! Spirit, soul, and body, may you be kept without break or blame till the arrival of our Lord Jesus Christ" (MOFFATT). "Without break!" "Without blame!" Here are two suggestive thoughts in the modern translation I have just quoted. "Without break" can indicate our Godward relationship. There must be no break, no rupture, in our communion. We must strive for unbroken fellowship with the Lord. "Without blame" can cover our manward relationship. Fellowship, conduct, and testimony must be in full harmony with our profession of holiness. We must be consecrated through and through.

It will be noted that Paul thought of man as a tripartite being: a trinity in unity. He is made up of spirit (life upward), soul (life inward), and body (life outward).

The body of the believer is the temple of the Holy Spirit

and must therefore be free of all pampering and excess and neglect. Everything associated with such a temple should contribute to the glory of God. Holy lips should plead His cause, far and near. Holy hands should be continually active, doing good. Holy feet should move incessantly, on errands of love and mercy.

The soul of the believer is the inner sanctuary, where all the powers of thought and imagination should be as priests serving the Lord. All unholy, lawless, roving thoughts must be banished. The Christian's conscience and self life must be disciplined by God's Word and Spirit, until they obey His dictates without a murmur.

The spirit of the believer must be guarded as the holy of holies. Pure worship and devotion and worthy thoughts of God must be cultivated. Worthy reverence and trust and conceptions of God must characterize the waiting, watching soul. If the saint is not to hang his head in shame and self-reproach as the Master asks questions of his secret soul, then every part of his complex nature must be sancitifed as His Coming draws near. With such a blessed hope in view, he must be more holy. And what God commands, He graciously supplies. He calls us to be wholly sanctified, and "Faithful is he that calleth you, who also will do it" (5:24). No wonder Saint Augustine prayed, "Give what Thou commandest—then command what Thou wilt."

John Masillon reminds us that "in the days of primitive Christianity it would have been deemed a kind of apostasy not to sigh for the return of the Lord." Dr. Grattan Guinness says:

> It cannot be denied that for three centuries the Church held the doctrine of the Premillennial Coming of Christ. I think I have gone through all the writings of the Fathers for three centuries pretty carefully, and I do not know an exception unless it be [Origen] the only early writer who was often heterodox.

If the apostles and fathers used the Coming of Christ as an incentive to holy living and diligent labor, is it not time for the church to return to the truth so prominent in their writings and witness? May grace be ours to hail the dawn as those who are fully right with God and with our fellowmen!

Conclusion

It now remains for us to gather a few scattered thoughts together and apply them, accordingly, to our hearts.

As we are free agents, up to the edge of the grave, this life is serious; for no one can roll off on another his responsibility. There is only one safeguard: faith in Christ and love for Him. The Bible places emphasis upon the solemnity of living. Jesus came to bestow life upon men, to cause them to fulfill the end of their existence. And so, here and now, upon this earthly plane, is our grand opportunity to serve God, to be true Christians, and to submit to the glorious mastership of Christ. No purgative will ever give any man the right to enter through the gates of the Celestial City. If the blood of Christ is not sufficient, the cleansing fires of hell will never fit a man for heaven. Here and now is the day of salvation, and through the acceptance, by faith, of God's salvation, we reach the only certainty regarding our destiny in the life to come.

And the grace of God lasts to the furthermost limit of our sojourn here below. Says Professor Salmond: "The mercy of God extends to the last hour of life. The grace of God may be efficacious with many as it was with the robber on the Cross. Death itself may be their purgatory." When men come to die, whether in battle or otherwise, we can never tell what intercourse their spirits had with God; whether they did or did not turn to Him for pardon and grace at last.

"There's life in a look at the Crucified One." What we do know is that, as long as sin is persisted in and as long as God's loving grace is resisted, the sinner and God occupy separate spheres.

And if we believe that men and women must be eternally banished from the presence of God, if they linger and die in their sin, it behooves us to present the Gospel of the grace of God prayerfully, earnestly, and believingly, agonizing lest any should miss so great salvation. Because of the sorrows and agonies the lost must endure, let us plead with them to "flee from the wrath to come."